Gurdjieff Was Wrong
But His Teaching Works

OREST STOCCO

Gurdjieff Was Wrong
But His Teaching Works

Copyright © 2016 by OREST STOCCO

All rights reserved. No part of this book may be reproduced or transmitted in any form or by any means without written permission of the author.

ISBN 978-1-926442-12-9

Edited by Penny Lynn Cates
Cover Design by Penny Lynn Cates

ALSO BY OREST STOCCO

NOVELS

The Golden Seed
Tea with Grace
Jesus Wears Dockers
Healing with Padre Pio
Keeper of the Flame
My Unborn Child
On the Wings of Habitat
What Would I Say Today If I Were to Die Tomorrow?

NON FICTION

The Summoning of Noman
The Pearl of Great Price
The Lion that Swallowed Hemingway
Why Bother? The Riddle of the Good Samaritan
Do We Have An Immortal Soul?
Letters to Padre Pio
The Sum of All Spiritual Paths
Just Going with the Flow
Old Whore Life
Stupidity Is Not a Gift of God
In the Shade of the Maple Tree
The Man of God Walks Alone

George Ivanovich Gurdjieff was one of the most influential spiritual teachers of the 20th Century. Born in the Caucasus in 1872 of Greek-Armenian heritage, Gurdjieff went in search of ancient teachings at an early age which he partly documented in his book *Meetings with Remarkable Men*. His quest led him to secret brotherhoods, from which he gleaned a radical system of self-transformation that he called "esoteric Christianity" which he brought to the western world and taught until his death in France on October 29, 1949. He is buried in the cemetery at Fontainebleau-Avon.

"Blessed is he who has a soul, blessed is he who has none, but woe and grief to him who has it in embryo."

G. I. Gurdjieff

A Word to the Wise

They say that life is what happens to you on your way to work, which is simply a metaphor for the surprising twist that your life can take when you least expect it; like how Gregory Peck became an actor, for example.

Gregory Peck was a pre-medical student at Berkeley University, California. One day a man came up to him and said: "I'm the director of the Little Theater, and I need a tall actor; and I've seen you on the campus and I wondered if you'd come and have a try."

This director, Edwin Duerr, whom Gregory Peck did not know, was life's messenger calling him to his personal destiny of service to life through acting; and, unconscious of his own destiny, Peck explained his serendipitous calling in words that make one smile: "And I don't know why I did; I just said, well, why not?" And the rest is history.

I've read many accounts of how one's life was changed by a serendipitous occurrence not unlike Gregory Peck's experience, and I'd even venture to say that the most successful people in their field have been guided to their destiny by the invisible hand of providence; which is exactly what happened to me with Gurdjieff's teaching.

One may well ask, who is this Gurdjieff anyway? I've never heard of him, so why should I care? And one would understand your indifference. But if there's one thing that I've learned about human nature, it's that we all love a good story; and I can assure you that the story of why providence introduced me to Gurdjieff's teaching is not only a good story, but a story that may just be what happens to you on your way to work, or somewhere else.

Wouldn't that be a lovely surprise?

Orest Stocco,
Georgian Bay, Ontario
Friday, October 30, 2015

Table of Contents

1. A Strange Story 1
2. The Call of Soul 16
3. Life Is Not *"Merde"* 27
4. Everyman/Noman 34
5. My Personal Situation 42
6. Roses/Thorns 49
7. The Way of Soul 55
8. The Secret Way of Life 64
9. Waking Up to the Shadow 74
10. My Call to Writing 85
11. The Way of the Dream 93
12. Practical Proof that Gurdjieff Was Wrong 107
13. The Fallacy of No Separate Self 116
14. When the Fat Lady Stops Singing 125
15. Becoming Spiritually Literate 131
16. Cathedral of My Past Lives 138
17. Pilgrimage and Penance 144
18. Squaring the Circle of My Life 149
19. The Story of Our Becoming 156
20. The Transcendent Self 164
21. The Essential Gurdjieff 168
22. A Place Called Sanctuary 173
23. Blazing My Own Trail 178

24. Cheating the Devil 182
25. Awakened Conscience 188
26. To Be, or Not to Be? 192
27. Gurdjieff, Jung, and Me 196

1. A Strange Story

THIS IS A STRANGE STORY. It is true, because it is the story of my life; not all of it, because I have neither the memory nor the talent to write the full story of my life—and neither does anyone else, for that matter; it's the story of how I managed to do the impossible, or "square the circle" as they say in philosophy, but how to tell it?

I cannot tell it chronologically, because I just don't have the memory for the details of my life, and I did not keep a daily journal or diary, as many writers tend to do; so it seems that I have two choices: write my story as a novel memoir, which would grant me the creative freedom to tell my story, but instead of enhancing the veracity of my story, which literature does naturally by virtue of its aesthetic (*"Art is the truth above the facts of life,"* said Karen Blixen), it would seriously tax the credibility of my story; or I could tell it from my 20/20 perspective, and by this I mean from the perspective of knowing everything that I know about my life today that would shed light upon my strange but true story.

I've told my story in bits and pieces in all of my books, both my novels and books of letters, spiritual musings, and memoirs; but they don't satisfy the writer in me who has been called by that mysterious voice that calls all writers to the stories they are meant to write, and not until they write their story will they be satisfied.

The call this time was different, because it called me to tell *the* story of how I did the impossible to "create" my own soul, as Gurdjieff's teaching promised; and as much as I did not want to heed the call for the demands I knew it would make upon me (re-live experiences that I have resisted writing about because they are much too painful), out of love and respect for the man whose teaching saved me from having to repeat my life over again—which, according to 20/20 hindsight would be my third parallel life, *and living my same life over again twice has been more than enough for me!*—I have to heed the call and tell the story of how George Ivanovich Gurdjieff came into my life to save me from myself.

I said that this would be a strange story, and what could be stranger than living one's same life over again? This is a whole new perspective on reincarnation, which I had not heard of until it was revealed to me four years ago by St. Padre Pio during one of ten spiritual healing sessions that I had with a psychic medium who channelled St. Padre Pio that became the basis of my novel *Healing with Padre Pio;* but I will say more about this later. For now I simply want to introduce the concept of parallel lives to make the point that I came back to live my same life over again to achieve a different outcome, because I was not satisfied with the first outcome of my lifetime as Orest Stocco.

In short, I blew my opportunity to "square the circle" the first time I lived my life as Orest Stocco, and I was reborn into my same life to do what I failed to do the first time; and I have Gurdjieff to thank for fulfilling my Sacred Contract this time, because his teaching initiated me into the mystery of how to "create" my own soul.

I have put "create" in quotation marks, because strictly speaking one cannot create what one already is; and this is where my story begins, because with 20/20 hindsight I *know* that Gurdjieff was wrong to found his teaching upon the premise, however convincing it may be, that man is not born with an immortal soul.

Like an oak tree that sheds thousands of acorns, Gurdjieff told young Fritz Peters (*Boyhood with Gurdjieff*) at his Institute for the Harmonious Development of Man in Fontainebleau, France, maybe one acorn seed out of thousands will take root and grow into an oak tree; in like manner, out of thousands of newborn babies, maybe one will take root in life and "create" their own immortal soul if life provides the right conditions, and all the rest will go back to nature—*"merde,"* or shit as Gurdjieff crudely put it; but his teaching provided the opportunity for one to "create" their own soul, which is why he attracted so many followers, myself included. But what brought me to Gurdjieff's teaching? That's where my story should begin; or, more pertinent still, *why was I called to tell my strange story?*

Writing is a mysterious, if not mystical process. "Spooky," as the novelist Norman Mailer called it, which every creative writer will confirm if they are honest with themselves (*self-honesty* is central to my story, but I do not have sufficient context yet to do this concept justice); and not until a writer is ready to write their story will they be summoned by their creative unconscious to write it. Obviously then, I was ready; but what beckoned me to write my story?

Several days ago I was doing research online for my spiritual musing "The Shadow Personality," which I will post on my blog first and later include in my fourth volume of spiritual musings to be called *The Armchair Guru,* and I "chanced" (again, I draw a distinction by putting the word "chance" in quotation marks because I have come to believe that despite free will our life is choreographed and guided by signs, symbols, coincidences, and synchronicity), upon a You Tube radio podcast titled "In Search of the Miraculous featuring Laura Knight-Jadczyk," and I felt obligated to listen to it because *In Search of the Miraculous,* the book written by P. D. Ouspensky, was my introduction to Gurdjieff's teaching, and this podcast *compelled* me to explore Laura Knight-Jadczyk further.

For the next two days I watched all the You Tube videos and listened to all the interviews that I could find on Laura Knight-Jadczyk, and I listened with rapt attention to her expound upon her outside-the-box perspective on life and human nature, and I also read parts of her books thanks to Amazon's Look Inside Feature (I ordered her book *The Secret History of the World and How to Get Out Alive*); but it was her absolute conviction about human nature that alerted me to attention like a red flag to a bull, because I knew that she was no less wrong than Gurdjieff to believe that there are people in the world without a soul, and that's when I heard the clarion call to tell my story and set the record straight.

I was ready to tell my story or I wouldn't have been called, but I froze in terror at the prospect because I didn't want to go back there; and the only reason I opened up a new file in my word processor and wrote down the title that came to me—*Gurdjieff Was Wrong, But His Teaching Works*—was more out of literary curiosity than anything else, because I knew that if I got the entry point into my story it would be enough to induce me to write it; and the entry point was my first sentence, "This is a strange story," which was the best entry point of any story I had ever written, or read for that matter, and which met my literary mentor Hemingway's credo of always starting a story with "one true sentence," and I abandoned to my creative unconscious to tell the story of how I "squared the circle" and found my true self.

I have devoted many years of my life to writing and sacrificed many pleasures and personal obligations that cost me dearly, but I have cultivated a relationship with my creative self that has taken the mystery out of the "spooky art of writing," and when I abandon to my creative unconscious I engage what C. G. Jung, the man who was to become my personal hero, called the "transcendent function," and I can tell my story from the perspective of my transcendent self that will do my story all the justice it deserves.

So, what then brought me to Gurdjieff's teaching?

DESPERATION. That's what. When life can do no more for one to satisfy the longing in their soul to be more, the bottom drops out of their life and they fall into a pit of hopeless despair; and out of desperation they surrender to life, and then the merciful law of divine synchronicity responds, as it did for me…

DESPERATION and **SYNCHRONICITY**. These two words are joined at the hip, because desperation has the peculiar ability to set the merciful law of divine synchronicity into motion, and out of nowhere there appears in one's life an opportunity to pull oneself out of despair so one can continue on their journey to wholeness and completeness, as Robert H. Hopcke confirms with his book *There Are No Accidents, Synchronicity and the Stories of Our Lives*.

But I didn't need Hopcke or anyone else to confirm my conviction, because in my commitment to find an answer to the question that catapulted me into my quest for my true self (*who am I?*), I was spared the anxiety of my desperation by the merciful law of divine synchronicity every time I came to another dead end, and I call it a divine law because all the synchronicities that came to me in my most desperate times of need went so far beyond the laws of probability that they had to be providentially designed, which is why they always made me feel blessed and holy, and until science can prove otherwise I have to maintain my conviction that we are all guided by this benevolent "intelligence," which I first identified as the Way like Jesus but over time came to call "the omniscient guiding force of life."

"We Poets in our youth begin in gladness, /But thereof come in the end despondency and madness," said William Wordsworth in "Resolution and Independence," the poem that I turn to whenever I become possessed by the demon spirit of gloom and doom responsible for all those existential feelings of anxiety and despair, because in this poem Wordsworth unlocks the mystery of life; and the sanctifying grace of the poet's synchronicity that day lifts my spirits back up to where they belong in the uncomplicated joy of simply being alive.

After a night of heavy rain and roaring wind, the morning sun brought out all of God's innocent creatures, and the poet went out walking in the lonely moors "happy as a boy" when suddenly he has a turn of mind and becomes possessed by the demon spirit of gloom and doom, "And fears and fancies thick upon me came; /Dim sadness—and blind thoughts, I knew not, nor could name."

This is life. This is what it means to be human. This is the paradoxical nature of man. Out of nowhere, the demon spirit of gloom and doom floods our mind with feelings of anxiety and despair, and fear possess us, as it did the happy but now despondent poet; but then, out of nowhere, "whether it were by peculiar grace, /A leading from above, a something given," the lonely poet chanced upon an old man "Like one whom I had met with in a dream; /Or like a man from some far region sent, /To give me human strength, by apt admonishment," an ancient-looking Leech Gatherer conning ponds in the lonely moors to scratch out a bare sustenance, and as they talked the old man's words, "stately in the main" and "cheerfully uttered, with demeanor kind," drove away the demon spirit of gloom and doom that possessed the dejected poet, and Wordsworth ends "Resolution and Independence" with some of the most inspiring words in English poetry: "I could have laughed myself to scorn to find /In that decrepit Man so firm a mind. /'God,' said I, 'be my help and stay secure; /I'll think of the Leech Gatherer on the lonely moor!'"

Was it pure chance that Wordsworth came upon the old Leech Gatherer that morning when his demon spirit of despair possessed him—and by demon spirit I simply mean his *shadow personality*, which I will get into later in my story; or was his encounter with the Leech Gatherer providentially designed, as Wordsworth suggested in his poem?

And what about the extraordinary coincidence that Gurdjieff reveals in the last chapter of his unfinished book, *Life Is Real Only*

Then, When "I Am", the chapter so aptly titled "The Outer and Inner World of Man"?

But first, who was this man called Gurdjieff anyway? Who was this strange Armenian/Greek mystic whose last words to his followers before he died in Paris, France on *October 29, 1949*, four years after I was born in Calabria, Italy, were, "I leave you in a fine mess"? And that was the polite translation; the word he actually used was not the phrase "fine mess" but "*merde*," the French word for shit.

Intentionally blunt and to the point, that was Gurdjieff; the most no-nonsense, but yet one of the most compassionate people I ever had the pleasure of meeting vicariously through all the many books that I read on his life and teaching, a man whom I'm proud to call my mentor. But he was more than a mentor to me, and it is essential to my story that I explain exactly what I mean by this.

Suppose, for the sake of artistic clarity, "the truth above the facts of life" if you will—after all, as the American poet Adrienne Rich said, *"Poetry is an act of the imagination that transforms reality into a deeper perception of what is"*—we imagine someone lost in a maze, and for days, weeks, months, years, and lifetimes and he is looking for a way out; but he cannot find the exist. He is desperate. So desperate that he finally surrenders to his situation and whiles away in hopeless despair, declaring with philosophical conviction like the philosopher Jean Paul Sartre that "life is a useless passion."

Not unlike Camus's metaphor of Sisyphus condemned to his hopeless fate of forever rolling his rock up the hill in Hades, so too is our man trapped in the maze of life condemned to his fate of never finding his way out; but what if by some miracle someone comes along and says to him, "I can teach you how to find the way out," wouldn't he be more than simply a mentor to him?

It's tempting to use the word savior, but this would be the last thing that Gurdjieff would want to be called; because it wouldn't be true, and his teaching attests to the validity of this perspective. As Gurdjieff liked to say, **"I give you good leather, but you must make your own shoes."**

Gurdjieff gave me good leather, but I had to make my own shoes; that's why he's not my savior but more than a mentor. He was my teacher. But it was what he taught me that made him special; and what he taught me was how to take evolution into my own hands to

Gurdjieff Was Wrong But His Teaching Works

complete what nature could not finish. That's the secret of Gurdjieff's teaching and the mystifying power of the man who attracted seekers like bees to honey, especially disillusioned writers and artists that had exhausted their creative fire. But even Gurdjieff with all of his esoteric knowledge and gnostic wisdom was also guided by the merciful law of divine synchronicity, as he tells us in the concluding chapter of his final book *Life is Real Only Then, When "I Am."*

I re-read this book with an ironic smile as I re-acquainted myself with Gurdjieff's Work, which is what he called his Fourth Way teaching, because it had been almost forty years since I had moved on to another path to continue my journey through this world (which, incidentally, was also provided for me by the merciful law of divine synchronicity); but because I was called to tell the story of how I "created" my own soul with the help of Gurdjieff's teaching, I had to go back to all of my Gurdjieff literature (and I have a whole library on Gurdjieff and his teaching) to bring back the memories of my *conscious labor* and *intentional suffering* that I needed to "create" my own soul, and I smiled in irony because from my 20/20 perspective all the mystery of Gurdjieff's teaching evaporated like morning fog in the warming sun as I read through Gurdjieff's obfuscating verbiage in the last book of his long and tortured series, *Life Is Real Only Then, When "I Am."*

It was humorous, how difficult if not impossible Gurdjieff made it to ferret out the secret of his teaching because he believed that if it was handed out on a silver platter it would not be appreciated and of little value to self-development, which unfortunately was true as I painfully learned through years of *conscious labor* and *intentional suffering;* but once the secret way of life gave itself up to me, the irony of Christ's words that his teaching was only for those who had eyes to see and ears to hear made me laugh, because Gurdjieff called his teaching "esoteric Christianity," a teaching of self-transformation which can be summed up in one of Christ's most perplexing and paradoxical sayings: **"He that loveth his life shall lose it; and he that hateth his life in this world shall keep it unto life eternal."**

As disconcertingly simple as it may be (again, the irony is in coming to the realization of its simplicity, which can take one a whole lifetime of *conscious labor* and *intentional suffering* to realize), Gurdjieff's whole teaching is packaged in that one saying, because one cannot "create" one's own soul unless one "dies" to one's outer life—which brings me back to the concluding chapter of Gurdjieff's last book, "The Outer and Inner World of Man," and Gurdjieff's synchronicity.

But before I get to this, let me take some of the mystery out of what Gurdjieff meant by calling his teaching "esoteric Christianity," because this has puzzled every writer who has tried to ferret out the secret of Gurdjieff's teaching…

In the *Gospel of Thomas* Jesus said, **"Whoever finds the interpretation of these sayings will not taste death."** I broke the code of Christ's sayings and found the correct interpretation, which can only reveal itself as one lives the sayings. This is what Jesus meant when he said, **"Therefore whosoever heareth these sayings of mine and, and doeth them, I will liken him unto a wise man, which built his house upon a rock"** (Math. 7: 24). By "rock" Jesus meant one's own immortal soul, which is exactly what Gurdjieff meant by "creating" one's own soul through *conscious labor* and *intentional suffering*. DOING is the operative word then in both Christ's and Gurdjieff's teachings, because without making the *conscious effort* to transform the consciousness of one's outer self, one will never transcend himself.

This puzzled me for a long time, because Gurdjieff implied that Christ's teaching was all about "creating" our own soul too; and even though in one sense it is about "creating" our own soul, strictly speaking it's more about what Jesus specifically referred to as being born anew—which was no less puzzling back then, as the man called Nichodemus revealed to Jesus, as it still is today—

"Marvel not that I said unto you, Ye must be born again," said Jesus to Nichodemus. **"The wind bloweth where it listeth, and thou hearest the sound thereof, but canst not tell whence it cometh and whither it goeth; so is everyone born of the Spirit"** (Math. 3: 7-8). But Nichodemus did not understand, and replied "How can these things be?"

Nichodemus could not fathom returning to his mother's womb to be born again, because he could not "see" that Jesus was referring to his spiritual birth; and the secret of both Christ's and Gurdjieff's teaching lies in the mystery of this spiritual second birth, which can only be realized through what Jesus referred to as ***"dying to one's life to save one's life,"*** and Gurdjieff referred to as "creating" one's own soul through the *conscious labor* and *intentional suffering* of transforming oneself; and not until one actually *has* the experience of this spiritual second birth will one be initiated into the deep secret of Christ's and Gurdjieff's teachings.

I did; that's why I was called to tell my story. But it's too early to reveal how I "created" my own soul and gave birth to my spiritual self. For now I just want to clear up the confusion that Gurdjieff created when he called his teaching "esoteric Christianity." Both teachings refer to the same process of spiritual self-realization consciousness by practicing a specific way of life; and it is this specific way of life that I labored indefatigably to realize when the merciful law of divine synchronicity called me to Gurdjieff's teaching by way of Ouspensky's book *In Search of the Miraculous* in my second year of philosophy studies at university when I fell into deep despair when I realized that philosophy could do no more for me.

"When the student is ready, the teacher appears," says the old saying; and I was ready for a new teacher because philosophy had brought me as far as it could take me in my quest for my true self, and in my third year I dropped out of university with nothing but Gurdjieff's perplexing teaching to guide me. But I will get to this part of my story later; for now I just want to provide the context for the synchronicity that Gurdjieff experienced while writing the concluding chapter "The Outer and Inner World of Man" for his last book *Life is Real Only Then, When "I Am."*

Gurdjieff got stuck working on his last chapter, as all writers get stuck when they have been brought as far as their creative unconscious can take them; and that's when the merciful law of divine synchronicity stepped in to help him.

This was the concluding chapter of his long and protracted series of books (the first was *All and Everything, Beelzebub's Tales to his Grandson* and the second *Meetings with Remarkable Men*) that he had set upon to write to pass onto the world his system of self-transformation in the hope of waking man up from the "hypnotic sleep of life," so he had to get it right; but he couldn't. For days he worked on his last chapter, but it would not come; and he pondered, and pondered.

Gurdjieff's dilemma was how to show the distinction between the outer and inner world of man, a distinction that would put his teaching into perspective so everyone could see through the "madness" of all that *conscious labor* and *intentional suffering* that was necessary to "create" one's own soul, which Gurdjieff obfuscated by metaphorically alluding to in his last chapter as "the problem of the prolongation of human life," when to his surprise the merciful law of divine synchronicity stepped in to help him—which was the first providential coincidence that helped clear the way for the miraculous synchronicity that would complete the final chapter and his life's work.

Gurdjieff was at Child's café in New York City when he was working on the last chapter of *Life Is Real Only Then, When "I Am,"* which is where he did most of his writing when he was in New York; and, of course, he was surrounded by some of his devoted followers drinking coffee, talking, and soaking in the aura of their teacher as he worked on his book. One of the men sitting was a writer who had translated Gurdjieff's writing into English, and Gurdjieff asked him to translate what he had just written so he could see how the book would sound.

Gurdjieff listened attentively, but when he heard that the man had translated his phrase *"intentional suffering"* with the phrase *"voluntary suffering,"* he objected; and they got into a heated discussion, because Gurdjieff wanted him to see the distinction between *intentional* and *voluntary suffering*. And that's when the divine law of synchronicity stepped in to resolve Gurdjieff's dilemma: one of the group was called to the telephone, and he came back to inform everyone that Alfred R. Orage, one of Gurdjieff's most loved and respected teachers of his system had just passed away; and soon everyone paid their respects and condolences to Gurdjieff for the great loss of one of the most efficient transmitters of his teaching who was loved and respected by everyone and whom Gurdjieff called "my brother."

For days and weeks people came up to Gurdjieff at Child's café to pay condolences for the passing of Gurdjieff's close friend and teacher of his system, but Gurdjieff couldn't help notice how shallow and insincere many people were because some didn't even know Orage; and Gurdjieff saw the meaningful connection with his chapter and decided to use their shallowness and insincerity to show the distinction between the outer and inner world of man, the fundamental theme of his teaching and the books that he was writing—thus setting up the conditions for the synchronicity that brought his life's work to literary closure...

So, just what is this great distinction that Gurdjieff wanted to make between *intentional* and *voluntary suffering*? Why was it so important that the merciful law of divine synchronicity had to intervene to help Gurdjieff explain the distinction in his closing chapter for the followers of his enigmatic teaching?

In a word, the distinction is one of effort; and the best way to illustrate what I mean by effort would be by way of analogy, one which I experienced when I took up long distance running while I was living Gurdjieff's teaching with such passionate commitment that it had become almost pathological.

One summer day as I was running down Highway 11 along the shoreline of Lake Helen in my hometown of Nipigon, Northwestern Ontario, I had to make extra effort that day to build up the momentum for my seven mile run; and the more effort I endeavored to make (*intentional suffering*), the more I realized that I had to run *with* my legs and not *on* my legs, because running *on* my legs was passive running while running *with* my legs was active running. And the more *intentional effort* I made to run *with* my legs and not *on* my legs, the more conscious I became of running because it was now *intentionally purposive;* whereas when I slackened my attention and ran *on* my legs, I was less conscious of running because it wasn't as *intentionally purposive*, and this was not as satisfying as conscious, active running.

This is why I created a new term for holistic running, which I called *metabiological running*; because conscious, active running created more "virtue" than passive running did; and by "virtue" I mean that special energy that I needed to "create" my own soul. And this speaks to the central mystery of Gurdjieff's teaching, because it takes this special kind of energy to "create" one's own immortal soul.

To re-enforce my perspective on the distinction between *intentional* and *voluntary* effort, let me illustrate this distinction with another image that has just come to me of a large bull moose running across an open field. I was on my way one day to the city of Thunder Bay to pick up supplies for my work (I had started my own house-painting business when I dropped out of university) when I noticed a large bull moose step out from the woods into the open field of Welsh's Farm along the Trans-Canada Highway.

It stood still as it surveyed the open field, and then it began to trot across to get to the woods on the other side; but it was how it moved that arrested my attention: it was magnificent in its stride, giving me the impression that its whole body moved with conscious intention, its powerful legs lifting and landing like pistons on the old steam locomotives, and I had to pull over to admire the beautiful creature.

Actually, now that I reflect upon this image, it was how this moose trotted across the open field with what I felt to be conscious intention that gave me my insight on running *with* my legs instead of *on* my legs; and I don't think I'm embellishing my memory by saying that this moose was responsible for helping me to see the distinction between *voluntary* and *intentional* effort, as I did every day after work when I went for my run from St. Sylvester's Church to Five Mile Park along the shores of Lake Helen.

Of course my running was voluntary, because I didn't have to go for a run every day; but it was *intentional* insomuch that I wanted to incorporate my running into my Gurdjieffian discipline of "work" on myself, so I had to make the effort—especially when I was overtired from work or when the weather was miserable; and the image of that magnificent moose running across the open field with the purposive intention of getting to the woods on the other side inspired me to run with *conscious, intentional purpose*, which underlined Gurdjieff's distinction between *intentional* and *voluntary suffering*—the dynamic engine of "work on oneself" that was central to his teaching of "creating" one's own soul.

Years later I had a dream that confirmed the *metabiological* benefits of my long distance running, but I will relate this dream when my story has more context; I mention it now simply to confirm that my own life was my "institute for the harmonious development of man," and distance running became such a big part of my life that like the "guru of running," Doctor George Sheehan (*Running and Being*) I could also shout, *"In running I found my salvation!"* But this also requires an explanation, which I will give when I relate the dream that put my running into perspective with the Gurdjieffian path that I was carving out for myself with his teaching of "work on oneself."

So there was Gurdjieff, nearing the end of his life trying with superhuman effort to pass on his teaching with as much calculated clarity as he could muster in the last chapter of his final book *Life Is Real Only Then, When "I Am"* but who hit a brick wall because he could not figure out a way to make it clear for the reader that the fundamental purpose of his teaching and life's mission was to extend the life of mortal man by teaching him how to "create" his own immortal soul.

The date was *April 10, 1935,* and Gurdjieff, with "extraordinary effort" worked and reworked the beginning of his last chapter, and not until the evening of the next day did he begin to get an inkling of how to give expression to the central theme of his teaching, which he called his "clue," and it came to him when he read over what he had written and came to the expression "the problem of the prolongation of human life"—but it was not enough to break through into the clarity he sought, and he decided that he had to make it absolutely clear what position "present-day science" held on the question of "the prolongation of human life."

He thought and pondered and reflected until *April 4th* how to introduce science's understanding of the issue on how to "prolong human life," but to no avail; and, he said, "It became absolutely clear to me that without such an introductory theme everything else would have no worth at all."

In other words, if he could not show the limitations of science on the issue of the "prolongation of human life" his teaching of how to "create" one's own immortal soul would have "no worth at all," and that's when the merciful law of divine synchronicity intervened to give him exactly what he needed to bring closure to the final chapter of *"Life Is Real Only Then, When "I Am"*

It was early Sunday morning, and rather than try to sleep, which he couldn't do all night long as he wrestled with his problem, he decided to go for a stroll in the city. It was very early, but he saw someone moving in the street and realized it was a newspaper vendor; so he bought a copy of *The New York Times*. But as he paid the vender he realized it was in English, and he didn't have enough command of the language to read it with satisfaction; so he asked the vendor if anyone else in the neighborhood had European papers, for example Greek, Armenian or Russian.

The vendor gave him directions to the Jewish district where they sold Russian newspapers, and Gurdjieff bought a copy of each of the two Russian papers; and he went to his room and lay down on his bed and started to read one of the papers. But, as he writes in his last chapter, "All the articles were so 'honeyed' that I put it down and picked up the second," and that's when the merciful law of divine synchronicity stepped in: "As I opened it, the first thing on which my eyes fell was this title—'The Problem of Old Age,' that is, just that question which for the course of three days and nights had left me no peace."

The paper was the *Russky Golos*. The date was Sunday, *April 14, 1935*. The article was titled "The Problem of Old Age," written by P. Mann; and Gurdjieff includes the entire article in his last chapter (translated into English) to make his point that "present-day" science was at its limits and could not solve "the problem of the prolongation of human nature," thereby giving Gurdjieff the peace of mind to provide his readers with a system that would help man—*if he took the requisite initiative*—to prolong his mortal life by "creating" his own immortal soul; and Gurdjieff brings literary closure to his life's mission with the following words:

"And thus, every man, if he is not just an ordinary man, that is, one who has never consciously 'worked on himself,' has two worlds; and if he has worked, and has become a so to say 'candidate for another life,' he has even three worlds."

Meaning, that with "work on oneself" man will have an outer world, an inner world, and a third higher world "created" out of his outer world and inner world; but, as usual, Gurdjieff obfuscates clarity with tortured verbiage, and to bring the first chapter of my strange story to closure let me endeavor to take the mystery out of Gurdjieff's teaching by reducing it to its simplest terms.

Gurdjieff called the last chapter of his final book "The Outer and Inner World of Man" because he wanted to draw attention to the dual consciousness of man, the outer and inner self—C. G. Jung's

Personality No. 1 and Personality No.2, which I will get to into later in my story. Gurdjieff pointed out with excruciating detail the false nature of our outer self with the shallowness and insincerity of the people who paid their condolences to him for the loss of his close friend Alfred R. Orage, deftly illustrating what Gurdjieff referred to as man's *"false personality,"* which set the stage for him to reveal the "clue" to his teaching—how to "prolong" our life by transforming the consciousness of our *false personality* by "working" on ourselves with *conscious labour* and *intentional suffering.*

This is how we can go to where our science still has not evolved to yet and take evolution into our own hands to complete what nature cannot finish by "creating" our own soul; and this brings me to my own archetypal *false self* and traumatizing sexual experience that I had in my early twenties that catapulted me into my quest for my *true self…*

2. The Call of Soul

When Soul calls, you cannot say no; because if you do, you will suffer like you have never suffered before as you are dragged kicking and screaming by the immutable forces of your life's essential purpose.

I was called by Soul, but I refused to heed the call and I suffered like I never suffered before: I was severed from my life by a sexual experience that brutally shocked my conscience awake, and out of self-revulsion and guilt I had to go on a quest for my *true self,* because the person who did what he did that awful night was not me; and that's what brought me to Gurdjieff's teaching...

I never cease to marvel at how the merciful law of divine synchronicity works, especially when I'm working on a new book, because it always seems to invite coincidences into my life like pennies dropped from heaven to assist me in my new creative endeavor; and no sooner did I bring the first chapter of this story to closure and the heavens dropped my second chapter "The Call of Soul" into my lap by way of a movie on TV called *Love and Savagery* that I "chanced" upon when I went downstairs for lunch upon bringing my first chapter "A Strange Story" to closure.

I had seen *Love and Savagery* before, and I loved the movie because it illustrated with poignant clarity the "love and savagery" of this mysterious calling that people get when they are ready to proceed to the next stage of their destined journey; but this requires an explanation that may be dangerously presumptuous so early in my story because it presupposes my whole life's quest and could easily tax the reader's credulity, but I have no choice: I am impelled by my *inner self* to take the risk, for which I have a workable precedent that lends support to my incredible boldness.

When I came back from France where I had gone to begin my quest for my *true self* after divesting my interest in the pool hall and vending machine business that I operated for several years, I worked for a year selling for University Scholarship of Canada before going to Lakehead University in Thunder Bay to study philosophy; and the salesman who trained me employed the technique of hitting his customers between the eyes and shocking them with the price it was going to cost them for the investment fund for their child's higher education, and then he eased the pain of the cost by pointing out all the benefits they would receive.

This was a very effective technique which I mastered, but over time I began to notice that I was selling myself and not the investment fund for their child's university education, and I began to hate myself. But because of my literary interests, I was familiar with Arthur Miller's play *Death of a Salesman,* which years later was made into a movie starring Dustin Hoffman, and I had no desire to end up an empty shell of a man like the desperate Willy Loman; so I quit my job selling and decided to go to university to study philosophy.

It was a strange feeling, selling myself to win my customer's confidence; but I was a handsome young man with curly hair, charming, and very affable, and I used everything that I had to make my sale. It was very seductive at first, but I soon began to feel the weight of my inauthenticity (my *false self*) upon my conscience; and I had to quit selling or suffer the highly probable consequence of becoming like Willy Loman. *And some people have the nerve to say that literature doesn't make a difference!*

So if I may, then; let's say that I'm selling you an investment fund for your higher education, and I'm going to state at the outset of my strange story that the reason I *know* that Gurdjieff was wrong to found his teaching upon the premise that man is not born with an immortal soul is because I had an experience with a past-life regressionist many years after I "created" my own soul that brought me back to the Body of God where all new souls come from, but I was a soul without a reflective self-consciousness, or an individual "I", and in the same regression I went back to my first primordial human lifetime as a higher primate where I gave birth to my own reflective self-consciousness, the "I" of our immortal spiritual nature. I actually re-experienced the birth of my reflective self in my regression.

So there it was; a *personal experience* that proved conclusively that new souls come from the Body of God without a sense of self; and as these new souls evolve through the natural evolutionary process of life from lower to higher life forms they take in more and more *life force*, which I had learned from a previous experience that I had when I first began living Gurdjieff's system was the *"I Am"* consciousness of Soul, or the "I" of God; and the more *life force* that the new soul takes in from one life form to the next, the more *"I Am"* consciousness it will constellate, until one day, as I experienced in my regression to my lifetime as a higher primate, the constellated *"I Am"* consciousness attains a certain specific gravity and becomes aware of itself for the very first time in that new soul's earthly existence; and with the birth of a new "I" of God the new soul now has a rudimentary sense of self that separates it from its group consciousness to begin its individuation through the natural process of creating and resolving its own personal karma through new life experiences with each new incarnation—which I confirmed for myself with seven past-life regressions that I had when Penny and I moved to Georgian Bay.

So souls evolve in the consciousness of their own identity from one lifetime to the next until the natural process of evolution through karma and reincarnation can do no more for them, which is why the ancient alchemists said that man must complete what nature cannot finish; and that's when one is called to their spiritual destiny of realizing wholeness and completeness of self, as I illustrated in my last book *The Pearl of Great Price.* We are all called to our spiritual destiny, then; and this call comes throughout our evolution in one lifetime or the next, because the omniscient guiding force of life (the *"I Am"* consciousness of God) seeks to realize itself through the individuation process of our own evolving self-consciousness. And when we have outgrown one way of life and are ready for a higher path to greater self-consciousness, Soul calls us to our destiny like it did the Irish young lady in the movie *Love and Savagery* who was called to the nunnery.

But the call of Soul always comes with a costly price, because it demands the sacrifice of letting go of the life we know but have outgrown because it can do no more to satisfy the longing in our soul to be more; like the sacrifice Cathleen in *Love and Savagery* had to make by letting go of her newfound love for the young geologist/poet Michael whom she met one summer in her hometown of Ballyclochan on the west coast of Ireland.

Gurdjieff Was Wrong But His Teaching Works

Cathleen and Michael fell in love, and Cathleen was now torn between her love for God and Michael; and Michael put her in the awful position of having to choose between him and going to the nunnery to serve her Lord Jesus.

That's the "savagery" part of the call of Soul, but no one can escape the pain and suffering that it will cost us if we do not heed the call; because if one does not heed the call the ineluctable forces of our spiritual destiny will have no choice but to drag us yelling and screaming to our *true self*—which is what the ancient Greek Stoic philosopher Cleanthes implied in his *Prayer to Zeus*:

> Lead me, Zeus, and you too, Destiny,
> To wherever your decrees have assigned me.
> I follow readily, but if I choose not,
> Wretched though I am, I must follow still
> Fate guides the willing, but drags the unwilling!

As painful as it will be then, it will be much easier on us if we heed the call to our *true self* willingly, like Alfred R. Orage did when he heard the call to his higher path in Gurdjieff's teaching. But it still cost him to let go of his *New Age* magazine that he loved dearly but had outgrown because the intellectual path of reason and creative literature could no longer satisfy the longing in his soul to be all that he could be, as we learn in *A. R. Orage, A Memoir* by Philip Mairet:

"Between forty and fifty years of age most men, perhaps all, experience something of a crisis. They pass through the change from the upward to the downward arc of life, when something deep in the soul turns backwards towards home, whatever outward habits may be continued. They hear a whisper within, that they had better try some other mode of living, do something even opposite to what they have done before, and if they cannot bear to harken, they often die. Orage had lived by the steady, continual reinforcement of his quality of intellectual clarity, and it was a masculine, self-dependent, and solitary style of life. He now wanted, or rather needed, to give up, not indeed that quality, for it was his splendor and unique attainment, but the psychic striving that was mixed with it and was straining it to death. In a word, he wanted resignation, submission; and his renunciation was to give up all ambition and go to Fontainebleau as to a monastery" (*A. R. Orage, A Memoir* by Philip Mairet, p. 88).

The little town of Fontainebleau, France was where Gurdjieff had established his Institute for the Harmonious Development of Man, and Alfred Orage had been introduced to Gurdjieff's teaching through P. D. Ouspensky who had broken away from Gurdjieff and was teaching Gurdjieff's system privately in London; and the call of Soul for a higher path was so strong that Orage, whom the playwright George Bernard Shaw called the most brilliant editor of the century, sold his *New Age* magazine and went to Fontainebleau and became Gurdjieff's pupil for the rest of his life.

When his secretary of ten years of devoted service Alice Marks asked Orage, heartbroken and feeling like it was the end of the world for her, "But why must you go?" Orage could only answer, "I am going to find God."

Orage wasn't being poetical, because the call of Soul is a call from God; and he was much too honest with himself to not heed the call because the way of the intellect, however brilliant (and Orage published some of the most brilliant writers of his time—Shaw, H. G. Wells, T. S. Eliot, and the gifted short story writer Katherine Mansfield who also became a student of Gurdjieff at his Institute) could no longer nourish his hungry soul with his mind; that's why he sold his magazine and went to Fontainebleau just as I had to sell my interest in the pool hall and vending machine business and go to Annecy, France—but I did not heed my call with dispassionate reason as the great editor Orage did; I had no choice. I could not live with what I had done and fled to France to get away from my life in Canada.

"I'm going away to look for something that I know lies in my own back yard, but I have to go all the same," I remember writing in a notebook; and, ironically, when I returned to Canada a year later and went to university to study philosophy it was on a walk through my own back yard to the CN railroad tracks and on to the breakwater in the Nipigon River where I got the inspiration for my *Royal Dictum* that opened up Gurdjieff's teaching that gave me what I had gone away to find; but suffice to say for now that I was severed from a life I had outgrown and had to go on my quest for my true self, because the longing in my soul to be all that I was destined to be could no longer be denied; and once I accepted my destiny I vowed to find my *true self* or die trying.

When C. G. Jung, the eminent Swiss psychiatrist and co-founder with Sigmund Freud of depth psychology with his discovery of the collective unconscious, turned forty he was called by Soul to change his life or suffer the consequences. Feeling the unbearable anguish of his spiritual longing, he had no choice but to heed the call and he went on the hero's journey to find his lost soul, which he recorded in his Black notebooks that he later transcribed with illustrations into what became *The Red Book*, the chronicle of his heroic journey:

"At that time, in the fortieth year of my life, I had achieved everything that I had wished for myself. I had achieved honor, power, wealth, knowledge, and every human happiness. Then my desire for the increase of these trappings ceased, the desire ebbed from me and horror overcame me... 'My soul, where are you?' I speak, I call you—are you there? I have returned. I am here again..." (*The Red Book*, A Reader's Edition, p. 127).

Jung had returned, but where was he? Obviously—*well, it's not that obvious, otherwise life wouldn't be the mystery that it is!*—he was out in the world achieving "honor, power, wealth, knowledge, and every human happiness," but he achieved his life's goals at the expense of his inner self. As Jung put it in his memoir *Memories, Dreams, Reflections*, he had to grow in Personality No. 1 (his outer self) to achieve his worldly goals, but he did so at the expense of his Personality No. 2 (his inner self); and by the time he turned forty he began to feel how far he had distanced himself from his inner self, and he was called to find his lost soul or suffer the unbearable anguish of his own nothingness, as he tells us in what he eventually came to call his "confrontation with the unconscious":

"He whose desire turns away from outer things, reaches the place of the soul. If he does not find the soul, the horror of emptiness will overcome him, and fear will drive him with a whip lashing time and again in a desperate endeavor and a blind desire for the hollow things of the world. He becomes a fool through his endless desire, and forgets the way of soul, never to find her again. He will run after all things, and will seize hold of them, but he will not find his soul, since he would find her only in himself..." (*The Red Book,* A Reader's Edition, p. 129)

Such is the "love and savagery" of the call of Soul, the compelling need to heed the call and the sacrifice of letting go of one's worldly accomplishments (the desires of the outer self) to look for what one needs to satisfy the longing in his soul, a longing that can drive one to desperate measures—as it did the artist Jerry Wennstrom who burned all of his art and gave away his worldly possessions and went on a quest for his lost soul by placing his trust in God to guide him, and which he recorded in *The Inspired Heart, An Artist's Journey of Transformation*:

"As a spiritual path, art carried my life as far as it could within the limited scope of determined human effort and discipline. I knew I could not have given one more ounce of myself to art as worship and have survived. In retrospect, I honestly believe that my survival was at stake—certainly, survival of the spirit, perhaps my body as well. Ramakrishna has a wonderful parable about the vehicle of one's particular discipline. It goes something like this: When you take a boat across the river and you reach the other side, you do not drag the boat with you beyond that point..." (*The Inspired Heart*, Jerry Wennstrom, p.119).

Jerry Wennstrom's art had taken him as far as it could take him, to the other side of the river of his artist's life, and he knew in his heart that his art could not take him any further to satisfy the longing in his soul that art gave him; and desperate to find a new path on the other side of the river, he left his art and all of his worldly goods behind and abandoned his life to the mercy of God. "I trusted a higher good that I sensed was much better equipped to inform my choices than anything I had available in the limited range of will and intelligence," he wrote; and for fifteen years he lived his life totally dependent upon the merciful bounty of divine serendipity—*whatever he needed to survive, God always provided!*

Gurdjieff Was Wrong But His Teaching Works

The Inspired Heart is an incredible story of the modern hero's journey, a desperate artist in search of his own soul; and depending upon one's need to satisfy the longing in his soul, one will do *whatever* is asked of him to heed the call, as Jerry Wennstrom did—and as I did as well when I was "inspired" to create my *Royal Dictum* when I hit a brick wall with Gurdjieff's teaching of "work on oneself."

I was still in university. It was my second year. I had been given Ouspensky's book *In Search of the Miraculous* by a fellow student whom I had befriended in our English Literature class (he gave me the book as a gift when he returned to LU from his home in Toronto after the Christmas break; he told me that he "felt" the book was right for me, but not until many years later did I see his life-changing gift as an intervention by the omniscient guiding force of life), and I began to practice the Gurdjieffian discipline of "work on oneself" because this was what I felt I needed to satisfy the longing in my soul, but I couldn't quite "get it."

That's when I dreamt of Gurdjieff. I met him in a dream, and he was just as Ouspensky had described him—with powerful magnetic eyes and a gravitas that demanded attention and respect; but my need for guidance in my lonely quest for my *true self*, which philosophy was failing to provide for me because with every philosopher that I studied I felt more lost than found, was so great that I mustered my courage and asked Gurdjieff if he would accept me into his inner circle of special students.

"You not ready yet," Gurdjieff replied, in that matter-of-fact no-nonsense manner that he was noted for as I learned much later when I explored the Gurdjieff literature; and I woke up from my dream feeling sad and dejected. But upon reflection (*writing has a way of putting things into perspective*), I can see now that my dejection drove me to desperate measures, which was why I went for a walk the morning after I drove home to Nipigon to tend to family matters, and on my "philosopher's walk" down our back yard and on to the breakwater and little "island" in the Nipigon River I created my *Royal Dictum* that made me ready for Gurdjieff to accept me into his inner circle.

My *Royal Dictum* was my edict of self-denial that was "inspired" (again, I have to put this word in quotation marks because

I'm thoroughly convinced today of the omniscient presence of life's guidance force) by Sophocles' play *Oedipus Rex*, the story of how King Oedipus banished himself out of his kingdom of Thebes when he learned from his soothsayer Tiresias that he was responsible for the plague that had befallen his kingdom because of his heinous crimes of murdering his father in his arrogant youth and defiling his mother's bed by marring his father's wife who was Oedipus's mother.

I had gone on my walk to think things out, because philosophy, the "mother of all disciplines," wasn't doing what I had hoped it would, and after smoking half a dozen cigarettes on the little "island" as I pondered what Gurdjieff would have called my "terror of the situation," I started walking back because I could find no solution to my dilemma; but I was so desperate that I stopped on the breakwater a dozen or so yards from the mainland and looked up into the heavens and said, *"God, I know that we get nothing for nothing in this world, or any world for that matter; so please tell me, what price truth?"* and I waited, vainly hoping for an answer.

As I waited for God's reply, I stared at the fast-flowing water of the Nipigon River as it swept by the breakwater on its way to Lake Superior, and for some strange reason (again, I have to attribute this to the omniscient guiding force of life, which in this case I can simply call my Higher Self), Ecclesiastes came to mind, and I quoted the Preacher's words out loud: *"All the rivers run into the sea; yet the sea is not full; unto the place from whence the rivers come, thither they return again."* And no sooner did the Preacher "speak" to me, and my mind called up Sophocles' play *Oedipus Rex* and the price that he had to pay to get rid of the plague that had befallen his kingdom; and I took out my pocket notebook and wrote my *Royal Dictum*, which came straight from my creative unconscious: *"I am like Oedipus Rex. I am going to exile myself out of my own kingdom. I embrace my becoming blindly, and I leave all of my sins behind me. I am going to go against the natural course of evolution, and each obstacle that I encounter I will consume."*

My kingdom was the "kingdom of my own senses," and I vowed on the spot to deny myself all the pleasures of my private kingdom for the rest of my life for the truth that I sought, which was my *true self*; and the moment I stepped onto the mainland I threw my package of cigarettes away and began my long and painful journey of self-denial in my hope to getting back to the "source" of my life—my *true self*. And in my second year of living my edict of self-denial (Oedipus had passed an edict that whoever was responsible for the plague in his kingdom would be banished from his kingdom) I dreamt of Gurdjieff again, and he accepted me into his inner circle of special students.

In my dream, I was kneeling in front of the man whose teaching of "work on oneself" I had finally penetrated with my *Royal Dictum*, and we were surrounded by a circle of his closest pupils. Gurdjieff, his bald dome shining bright and his round face smiling like the sun, put his hands upon my shoulders and said, "You ready. I very proud," and I became a student of his inner circle in the inner world of my dreams.

But I would never have "gotten" Gurdjieff's teaching without my *Royal Dictum*, because my edict of self-denial transformed my consciousness enough for me to "see" and "hear" the omniscient guiding force of life that Gurdjieff called the Work, Jesus called the Way, the Sufis call the Path, Taoists call the Tao, and Carl Jung called "the secret way" in his commentary to Richard Wilhelm's translation of the Taoist text *The Secret of the Golden Flower*—the hidden ancient teaching of how to "create" one's own soul and realize one's divine nature: "…when I began my life-work in the practice of psychiatry and psychotherapy, I was completely ignorant of Chinese philosophy, and only later did my professional experience show me that in my technique I had been unconsciously led along *the secret way* which has been the preoccupation of the best minds of the East for centuries," wrote Jung in his enlightening commentary to *The Secret of the Golden Flower*.

As the Sufis say, every soul is its own way to God; and when one is ready for the next step on their journey to what Jesus called the "kingdom of heaven," wholeness and completeness of self, which Jesus also called "the pearl of great price," one will be called by Soul to a higher path; as Cathleen was in *Love and Savagery* with her call to the nunnery, as Alfred R. Orage was to Gurdjieff's teaching, and short story writer Katherine Mansfield whom I will talk about later, and Jerry Wennstrom who was called to a deeper connection with himself, and my hero C. G. Jung who played a big role in my life when I needed someone to free me of the unconscious hold that my

Roman Catholic faith still had upon me, and indeed, as everyone is called when their life, however rewarding it may be to their creature comforts, can no longer satisfy the longing in their soul…

3. Life Is Not *"Merde"*

To write this strange story of how I "squared the circle" and "created" my own soul I've had to go back to my Gurdjieff library, which is quite extensive because when I was in the throes of Gurdjieff's teaching I ordered every book on Gurdjieff that I could get from *Samuel Weiser, Inc.* in New York City to satisfy my hungry mind; but I have too much life in me now to see Gurdjieff in the same light as I did when I desperately needed his teaching to liberate myself from myself, and as much as I tried to resist how I felt about my inner and outer teacher as I re-read dozens of books on Gurdjieff and related literature, I couldn't keep the thought from breaking free from my creative unconscious, and I had to write a spiritual musing for my blog to work out how I felt about Gurdjieff on *Thursday, April 16, 2015*, more than forty years after I discovered Ouspensky's book *In Search of the Miraculous*:

The Terror of the Situation

On a walk the other day after my morning writing, I came to what can only be called an enlightened understanding of what Gurdjieff referred to as *"the terror of the situation."* George Ivanovich Gurdjieff, the mystic Armenian/Greek philosopher who brought a teaching to the western world in the early part of the 20th Century that he called by various names—"The Work, The Fourth Way, The System, the way of the sly man, and "work on oneself" and which I lived for many years—defined the state of world affairs as *the terror of the situation*, because it seemed to him that the world would inevitably destroy itself if it didn't change its ways; and changing its ways, according to the enigmatic Mr. Gurdjieff, was for man to wake up from the "hypnotic sleep of life"—his urgent call to free ourselves from the inner chaos in which we live, and to ask ourselves why we are here and what we might become; but on my walk to the viewing pod overlooking the waters of Georgian Bay I stopped in mid thought and said to myself, *"This terror of the situation thing is nonsense. Life is always in a state of flux, going from the positive to the negative and back again. This is the nature of the human condition, and the way it's meant to be!"*

And that's the subject of today's spiritual musing, to shed new light on this Gurdjieffian declaration that sends chills up one's spine every time one turns on the evening news, because it's time we stopped being held hostage to this field of negative thought that in his vaunted wisdom Gurdjieff called *the terror of the situation...*

What we believe is our window onto the world, and when Gurdjieff looked out the window of his belief system he saw that man was not born with an immortal soul; and it was his mission—whether self-imposed or not, no one can say for certain—to introduce the western world to a teaching that would assist man to "create" his own soul; but after years of "working" on myself with his teaching I not only "created" my own soul, but I came to an entirely different conclusion—that man is by nature spiritual in essence, and that our purpose in life is to evolve and grow in the understanding of our own divine nature.

How I came to this realization is a long story, which I'm working on in my book *Gurdjieff Was Wrong, But His Teaching Works*, so I cannot expound upon it here; but it behoves me to explain how I came to see what I did through the window of my own belief system, starting with four past-life recollection dreams in high school, seven past-life regressions that I had forty years later, and two other remarkable experiences that all added up to a view on life that negated Gurdjieff's belief that man is not born with an immortal soul but has the potential to "create" one if he has the courage to take the initiative with *conscious effort* and *intentional suffering*.

When I "chanced" upon Gurdjieff's teaching at university through Ouspensky's book *In Search of the Miraculous,*

Gurdjieff Was Wrong But His Teaching Works

Fragments of an Unknown Teaching I didn't know whether to believe Gurdjieff that man is not born with an immortal soul, but in his teaching I saw the means to satisfy my need to find my true self, so I embraced Gurdjieff instinctively; and it was only by dint of relentless effort in the Gurdjieffian discipline of *conscious effort* and *intentional suffering*—the fundamental techniques of his teaching—that I resolved the paradoxical nature of my *being* and *non-being* and "created" my own soul; but it was from my newfound state of consciousness that I came to see that Gurdjieff was wrong to believe that man is not born with an immortal soul, and my perspective on life changed dramatically.

Given his belief that man is not born with an immortal soul, there was an urgency about Gurdjieff's teaching that drove many followers to the brink of despair; and, according to Louis Pauwels' book *Gurdjieff*, some of his followers were even driven to take their own life. So not only was one haunted by *the terror of the world situation*, but also by the terror of one's own nothingness; and that's what always bothered me about Gurdjieff's teaching. But because I knew that his teaching worked, I made allowances; until my walk the other day, that is.

From the day I dropped out of university in my third year of philosophy studies because philosophy had cast me so far adrift in a sea of endless speculation that I feared getting lost and drowning, I made a vow to build my life upon the truth of my own experiences and not anyone else's—philosophers like Nietzsche, Sartre, and Camus who I admired and respected but could not follow; and with one experience after another as I "worked" on myself with Gurdjieff's teaching, I began to feel solid ground beneath my feet. And on my walk the other day, whether due to what I had just written I cannot say, I felt emboldened to stand my own ground and declare Gurdjieff wrong to terrorize the world with his belief system.

So, why do I have so much confidence in the ground of my own being to stop being held hostage to Gurdjieff's *terror of the situation*? That's the question I asked myself as I stared out into the open water of Georgian Bay.

Ironically, Gurdjieff himself answered this question in *Views from the Real World, Early Talks of Gurdjieff as Recollected by his Pupils*. In "Glimpses of Truth," he said: "Judge everything from the point of view of your common sense. Become the possessor of your own sound ideas, and don't accept anything on faith; and when you, yourself, by way of sound reasoning and argument, come to an unshakable persuasion, to a full understanding of something, you will have achieved a certain degree of initiation." This is why Gurdjieff told his pupils, "There is only self-initiation into the mysteries of life," and my self-initiation into the divine mystery of Soul gave me the confidence to refute Gurdjieff's claim to *the terror of the situation*.

From the day I stepped onto the Gurdjieffian path of "work on oneself," I put myself under the influence of those cosmic forces that assist every soul in their efforts to realize their destiny; and three or four years into Gurdjieff's teaching I had an unbelievable experience that made no sense to me at the time but which laid the foundation for what was to come many years later.

It was springtime, and I had come home for lunch. I was self-employed with my own contract painting business, so I could allow myself more time to relax after lunch; and I went into the back yard of our family home just to sit and soak in the sun.

I positioned my chair and leaned back and rested my head upon the warm stucco of our house, and I shut my eyes and let my mind wander. The spring sun felt wonderful after another one of our long Northwestern Ontario winters, and I don't know how or why it happened but I began to feel myself being pulled back through time. I didn't question what was happening, I just went with the experience; and I felt myself floating back through the days and weeks and months and years and centuries, millennia, and countless eons—*all the way back to when there was no life at all on Planet Earth!*

I could see our world, and it did not look like the beautiful blue orb that Carl Jung tells us that he saw in

Memories, Dreams, Reflections when he left his body after his heart attack and looked down on Planet Earth from ten thousand miles above; the world that I saw was dull and grey, with gaseous vapours rising up to mingle with the gaseous vapors in the sky.

And that's when the miracle happened. When the vapors from the Earth mingled with the vapors from the sky, they formed the first building blocks of life in the amino acids of their combined elements; and then I felt myself being sucked into the amino acids like a liquid being poured into a receptacle, and as I imbued the amino acids with consciousness I *experienced* the inception of life on Planet Earth! *I actually experienced the genesis of life on our planet!*

It took me more than forty years to come to an understanding of what happened that day in the back yard of our family home, but after I "created" my own soul (in Christ's terms, I gave birth to my spiritual self) a few years after I experienced the inception of life on Planet Earth, I had seven past life-regressions when Penny and I relocated to Georgian Bay, and in one of my regressions I had two more experiences that helped me connect the dots and see the big picture of Soul's evolution through the life process on Planet Earth.

In my fourth regression I went back to the Body of God where all new souls come from, and I experienced myself as an atom of God without reflective self-consciousness. I was conscious, but I had no self-consciousness. I was a happy soul without an "I". I knew that I was myself, but I was un-self-realized in the Body of God; and then I felt myself being pulled into the evolutionary process of life on Earth, and I experienced my evolution through the stages of life all the way up to my first primordial human lifetime. I was the alpha male of a small group of higher primates, and I grunted all the time to show my group that I was in control; and if they did not obey me, I beat them savagely into submission. And every time I grunted to keep them submissive, they forfeited their will to me; that's how I constellated enough of their will-to-be to give birth to my own wilful sense of self.

It wasn't a full-blown "I", but I experienced enough of a dawning of wilful self-consciousness to know that I was separate from my group, and from that moment on I felt the loneliness of my separateness and a yearning that drove me from one lifetime to the next that never went away until I gave birth to my spiritual self in my current lifetime with the help of Gurdjieff's teaching; but I didn't figure this out until I connected the dots with the genesis of life on Planet Earth, because the "I" that slipped into the first building blocks of life was the consciousness of Soul and our divine nature that initiated the life process and would continue to evolve until it gave birth to a new "I" of God, as I did in my first primordial human lifetime.

That's how I know that Gurdjieff was wrong to believe that man is not born with an immortal soul, and on my walk the other day I liberated myself from the paralysing negative field of *the terror of the situation*, because I knew that if we don't realize wholeness and singleness of self, as Jung referred to our divine self, in our current lifetime we will just keep coming back until we do, because this is the purpose of life on Planet Earth.

After writing my spiritual musing I edited and clarified it as best I could, given the metaphysical nature of my experiences; and then I re-read two or three more books in my Gurdjieff library, but the enigmatic Mr. Gurdjieff now came across to me as a man hell-bent on saving the world with his radical "messianic" Fourth Way teaching.

But from the perspective of our life today, *April, 24, 2015* (Gurdjieff died *October 29, 1949*), I cannot see any noticeable difference that his teaching has made to change *the terror of the situation*. If anything—and I say this with regret but no apology—Gurdjieff has only added to the confusion of our situation.

Given my own experience with Gurdjieff's teaching, I have no doubt that he changed the lives of many people, as many books in my Gurdjieff library attest to—*Our Life with Mr. Gurdjieff,* by Thomas de Hartmann; *Gurdjieff Remembered,* by Fritz Peters; *Venture with Ideas*, by Kenneth Walker; *Gurdjieff,* by Louis Pauwels; *The*

Gurdjieff Was Wrong But His Teaching Works

Unknowable Gurdjieff, by Margaret Anderson; *Undiscovered Country*, by Kathryn Hulme; *Journey Through this World*, by C. S. Nott; *What Happened In Between, A Doctor's Story*, by William J. Welch, M.D.; *The Gurdjieff Work*, by Kathleen Riordan Speeth; and *Gurdjieff: Making a New World,* by J. G. Bennett, to mention only a few of the many books written about Gurdjieff's influence—the sad fact remains that the central conviction of Gurdjieff's teaching that man's life is nothing but *"merde"* that fertilizes nature's garden unless man "creates" his own immortal soul still hangs over the whole Gurdjieffian movement like a dark cloud; which I find very tragic.

But I suppose that's why I was called to write my story, to bring some clarity to this remorseless issue. After all, who has the knowledge (esoteric or otherwise), the wisdom (gnostic or otherwise), and the audacity to contradict the Gurdjieffian perspective that our life is *"merde"* unless we immortalize it?

Not that people don't believe that we are not born with an immortal soul, countless millions *do* believe that we are born with an immortal soul; but can anyone nullify Gurdjieff's conviction that we are only born with the potential to "create" our own immortal soul and if we don't we're nothing but *"merde"*? That's why I was called to tell my story, because of my personal experience that negates the premise of Gurdjieff's teaching…

4. Everyman/Noman

"The real history of the world seems to be the progressive incarnation of the deity," wrote Carl Jung in one of his insightful private letters, which is why in the spiritual tradition of the Way of The Eternal that I studied and lived for more than thirty years after I moved on from Gurdjieff's teaching, it is written: "Man is as important to God as God is to man." Which is the core mystery of life, and the basic theme of my strange story.

But to proceed with my story of how I "squared the circle" and "created" my own soul, I have to rely once again upon my old selling technique of stating my case up front (*socking the reader right between the eyes, I'm afraid*) and get the most vital question of soul's miraculous ability to both *be* and *not be* at one and the same time out of the way, because this is the root cause of all this confusion that philosophers and mystics have been trying to come to grips with since the dawn of reason.

"I am what I am not, and I am not what I am," wrote Jean Paul Sartre, who worked out the dialectics of man's becoming in his philosophical tome *Being and Nothingness* that forced him by the sheer logic of dialectical reason to conclude that our life is a "useless passion," which was a little more dignified than Gurdjieff's offensive description of man being *"merde";* but that's only because the existential philosopher could not break the recurring cycle of the *enantiodromiac* process of the human condition, which was the essential purpose of Gurdjieff's teaching of "work on oneself," because the more "work" one did on oneself the more one transcended the consciousness of their *being* and *non-being* and "created" their own immortal soul. That was the bane of Sartre's incomplete philosophy of *Being* and *Nothingness* and the mystical power of Gurdjieff's transformative teaching of spiritual self-realization; but I would never have resolved the issue of the human condition had I not been possessed by my own *daemon* to do what I did that night that shocked my conscience awake and drove me to

look for my *true self* or die trying. And that's where my story should begin—with the unbearable agony of my own *non-being*...

Very early in life Carl Jung saw the distinction in our evolving self by recognizing the dual nature of human consciousness, which in himself he called Personality No. 1, and Personality No.2. I wasn't as conscious of myself as my hero was at that age, but I became aware of a change in my personality between grades nine and ten when my *non-being* burst out with *daemonic* fury in grade twelve with my poem *Noman* but which I could not puzzle out until long after I had resolved the paradoxical issue of my own *being* and *non-being* and "created" my own soul with Gurdjieff's teaching and my *Royal Dictum*.

Somewhere between grade nine and ten I began to feel a peculiar change in my personality that I simply could not fathom. For some strange reason, which I did not connect with my own and family shadow until many years later, I began to be possessed by an impulse to falseness. I simply couldn't help myself, whenever the circumstances called for me to pretend to be more than what I was, my impulse to be false kicked in; and this made me feel weird, and guilty. But over time I ceased to notice when it kicked in (rather, I noticed but quickly repressed the feeling), and I just went on with my shadow-affected teenage life.

Then in grade twelve our English Literature teacher, a rather eccentric man with short-cropped salt and pepper hair and an eye that twitched every time he lost his patience with us, asked us to write a poem for the year book. Only one poem would be selected, and we were free to write on anything we wanted; but never in his wildest dreams did Mr. MacKay expect to get a poem like the one he got from me.

I woke up one morning possessed by the spirit of inspiration, and my poem erupted out of me with *daemonic* fury; but unfortunately I no longer have a copy of *Noman*, and the only lines that I remember are the closing two lines which are so powerful that I can only reveal them after I have provided the proper context.

Someday I may solicit the assistance of a good hypnotherapist to help me recover my lost poem, because it was fraught with so much symbolic meaning that I would love to study that poem today from the perspective of having solved the riddle of the human condition, our essential purpose being to expand the consciousness of God; but I do however recall the narrative storyline of my poem, and only after some thought did it occur to me that *Noman* was set free from the depths of my unconscious because I had opened the trap door to the collective psyche of man with my "inspired" (providentially guided) reading of the medieval morality play *Everyman* several days (or perhaps weeks; it is too far back to remember precisely when I read the play) before writing my narrative poem *Noman*.

This Christian morality play *Everyman* must have touched my soul so deeply that my creative unconscious took this opportunity to wake me up to my spiritual dilemma, and I woke up one morning with a burning desire to write; and out of me spewed *Noman* in a torrential flood of inexplicable passion. I was totally possessed by my own *daemon*, and I experienced every word of my poem because I *was* Noman!

In the anonymous play *Everyman*, God sends his messenger Death to summon Everyman (every person in the world) for a reckoning; but Everyman is not ready to die, and he asks Death for more time to prepare himself to meet God.

Death refuses, and Everyman panics. He asks his friends (symbolized in the person Fellowship) to accompany him, but they turn him down; and he asks his family (Kindred and Cousin), but they too refuse; and then he asks Goods (the material possessions that he has stored), but Goods refuses also.

Now desperate, Everyman asks Good Deeds, who wants to accompany him but cannot because he is too weak (symbolizing that Everyman had not done many good deeds in his life); but Good Deeds introduces Everyman to his sister Knowledge, who can help him by taking him to Confession.

Everyman weeps with joy. Confession tells Everyman that he will give him the precious gift of penance if he will confess his sins. Everyman calls upon the Lord to forgive his sins, and then Knowledge informs him that Good Deeds is strong enough now to accompany him, telling Everyman that he is now prepared for eternity, and Knowledge outfits Everyman with the robe of contrition to wear on his journey to eternity. The robe signifies repentance.

Good Deeds introduces Everyman to Discretion, Strength, his Five Wits, and Beauty and asks them to accompany Everyman on his journey. Knowledge then tells Everyman that he must receive the last sacrament of the Church, which he receives, and Discretion, Strength, Five Wits, and Beauty go with Everyman to his grave but refuse to accompany him to the afterlife.

But Good Deeds says, "Nay, Everyman. I will bid with thee." Knowledge stays behind; only Good Deeds accompanies Everyman to the afterlife.

That's the story of *Everyman*. In my poem *Noman*, God's messenger informs me that God wants a reckoning, and I am brought to the Court of God. God says to me, "Noman, hast thou my fish's scale?"

I answer that I do not have it, and God sends me into the "abyss with four corners" (the world) to find the "fish's scale" and return it to God.

God imposes conditions upon my return to the "abyss with four corners." I am allowed only three days to search for the "fish's scale" in the "abyss," but it takes one whole day to search each corner of the "abyss." This means that if I do not find God's "fish's scale" within my allotted three days, I will have failed because there would still be one more corner of the "abyss" left to search.

So I go back into the world in search of the "fish's scale" (which I deciphered years later to mean my lost soul) in the first "corner." (The four corners of the "abyss" symbolize the four points of the compass: North, South, East, and West; and they also, as I later came to realize, symbolize the four planes of consciousness of the lower worlds of God—the physical, astral, causal, and mental planes). And at the end of the first day I hear God's booming voice: "NOMAN, HAST THOU MY FISH'S SCALE?"

I answer that I do not have it, and I proceed to look in the second corner. I don't remember what I found in the first corner, but it wasn't my lost soul; and once again, at the end of the second day God shouts: "NOMAN, HAST THOU MY FISH'S SCALE?" Again I say no, and proceed to the third corner.

Once again, I cannot remember what I found in the second and third corners (aside from a vague memory that had to do with my mother in the third corner), but at the end of the day God once again shouts down to me: "NOMAN, HAST THOU MY FISH'S SCALE?"

I do not have it, and I am summoned back to God's Court. I tremble before Almighty God as I wait for God to pronounce sentence. God condemns me to the fourth corner for all of eternity to find my lost soul, and as I fall from heaven into the "abyss" I shout with no less passion and anger than Milton's fallen angel:

"Open you vile, voracious, loveable sweet whore!
God, why hast thou forsaken me?"

Thus ends my mythic poem *Noman*, with me wandering throughout my little corner of the world in my hometown of Nipigon, Northwestern Ontario in search of my lost soul. This is a powerful waking dream, an eruption of the archetypal *false self* of man into the full light of conscious awareness, and like all big dreams that come from the collective unconscious it is fraught with such symbolic meaning that it took me years to make sense of it—*but only after I had found my lost soul!*

But why did I shout what I did as I fell from heaven? Why would I call life a "vile, voracious, loveable sweet whore"? I was a tender teenage virgin when I wrote this poem. Was this my "inspired" motivation for writing my book of spiritual musings, *Old Whore Life: Exploring the Shadow Side of Karma* many years later? Why was I so angry at life? Why was I so angry at God?

This is why I went to a gifted psychic medium for a spiritual healing with St. Padre Pio on *August 9, 2010* (followed by nine more sessions), because I had so much anger in me. I relate my experience in my novel *Healing with Padre Pio,* and I'm happy to say that St. Padre Pio did heal me of my anger issues with God and the Roman Catholic Church—which I learned were a carry-over from my morally debauched past lifetime in Paris, France where I was known as *"le salaud de Paris!"*

Although the Noman of my poem is the archetypal *false self* of every soul in the world (Everyman's Noman, or shadow self), it was specifically my *false self* as well; that's why my poem was fraught with such *daemonic* energy. Noman was the collective *false self* of all my past life personalities, the archetypal shadow of every personality that I have lived in this "abyss with four corners" that we call life, as well as Everyman's *false self.*

I *was* Noman, Everyman's archetypal shadow; and when I was condemned to the world for all eternity to find my lost soul, I symbolized Everyman's quest for salvation from the endless *enantiodromiac* pattern of the human condition (the recurring cycle of karma and reincarnation); hence the outrage that Noman expresses when he's condemned by God and falls from heaven, because Noman cannot understand how God could possibly be so unfair. It's like Noman was asking, "what have I done that God would condemn me forever to the fourth corner of the abyss?"

To answer that question—which we all ask in one way or another and can be summed up in the simple question, "Why me, God?"—I have to ask myself, *"What happened to me that made me so angry at God?"*

And the answer lies in my past lifetime as *"le salaud de Paris,"* the infamous "scoundrel of Paris" who corrupted women with sex, because the universal story of Soul's individuation through life is told through the individual life experience of every soul, and as *Noman* spoke my personal journey through life so too did it speak every soul's journey through the consciousness of their own *non-being...*

That's how I came to resolve the issue of the human condition that Sartre's dialectic could not resolve. *"I am what I am not, and I am not what I am,"* concluded Sartre, but by "working" on myself with Gurdjieff's teaching (and, of course, my *Royal Dictum*; not to mention the sayings of Jesus), I blended the consciousness of my *being* and *non-being* (in Christ's words, I made the two into one "with no hypocrisy") and transcended myself, thus "creating" my own immortal soul which I *actually* experienced one day while standing in the doorway of my mother's kitchen while she was kneading bread dough on the kitchen table.

We were just talking when for no apparent reason I became imbued with the most wonderful feeling that I was immortal and would never die. It stole upon me like a thief in the night, just as Jesus said it would. The feeling was so complete that it possessed me body and soul, and I simply *knew* that I was immortal; and from that moment on I could say, ***"I am what I am not, and I am not what I am; I am both, but neither. I am Soul."*** I had *become* my true self. And from that day on I have never again felt lonely. And this brought to closure an experience I had in Annecy, France that I never understood but *knew* in my heart would come true one day.

I hadn't been in my tiny one room apartment very long (I had been living in my friend's widowed mother's house for a month or so, where I ate horsemeat for the first time in my life), and it felt good to be on my own; but I was still trying to find my way out of my confusion from the shock of my departure to a foreign land, and I was still reeling from cultural shock, so I was desperately lonely when I went for a walk that afternoon; and when I returned to my apartment I sat at my table and wrote the following words that just came to me but which gave me the comfort that I needed in my most forlorn hour:

Steadfast and courageous is he, who having overcome woe and grief remains alone and undaunted; alone I say for to be otherwise would hardly seem possible, for one must bear one's conscience alone. He must fight the battle, and he must win the battle, odds or no odds. He must win to establish the equilibrial tranquility of body and soul, and sooner or later he will erupt as a volcano of unlimited confidence which will purpose his life thereafter. And having given birth to such magnificence he will no longer be alone alone, but alone in society; and he will see the mirror of his puerile grief in the eyes of his fellow man.

Those words burnt themselves into my mind, and although I wrote thousands of pages during my one year stay in Annecy (an experience in "automatic" writing that I am not ready to talk about yet; as well as my first novel called *This Petty Pace* that reflected my confused state of mind), these words which came to me straight from the core of my being gave me the confidence to continue my quest for my *true self* because they "foretold" my success, and whenever I felt at my lowest in my desperate search for my true self I recited these words to give me the strength and courage to continue.

And years later when I transcended myself in my mother's kitchen that summer day while she was kneading bread dough on the kitchen table, I gave birth to my spiritual self and accomplished what Gurdjieff promised with his teaching of "work on oneself," and I brought to pass what I had been "foretold" on what I can honestly say was the loneliest day of my life; and whenever I look into the eyes of my fellow man today I can see my own puerile grief, and my heart goes out to each and every soul because I know what this journey costs.

And now to some details of my life…

5. My Personal Situation

I was born *July 31, 1945* in Calabria, Italy; in a village called Panettieri. My father and eldest brother immigrated to Canada first, sponsored by my father's sister, and my mother and the rest of the family came the following year; and we settled in Nipigon, Northwestern Ontario where my aunt owned the International Hotel.

I was five when we came to Canada, and I'm the fifth child of eight, with four brothers and three sisters (my young brother and sister were born in Canada); but I never felt that I belonged in my family. I wasn't the black sheep, as such; but I was certainly the odd sheep of our family.

I just didn't fit in, and this bothered me growing up. One of my older brothers called me a little devil, which I never quite understood until many years later when I began "working" on myself and learned about what Gurdjieff called our false personality and Jung called our shadow self, but now it makes perfect sense to me.

I was mischievous, but not in a getting-into-real-trouble kind of way; just annoying in an overconfident, conceited kind of way, and which I now attribute to what I refer to in serious jest as my "vanity" gene.

My father was an unskilled laborer and had trouble holding a job, and it took years before I understood why. He never learned to speak English, and he always felt that people were talking about him, which I since learned many new immigrants suffer from; but my father's paranoia was fueled by closet drinking, and he made our life very difficult. It was not an easy life growing up.

Not only did I inherit my "vanity" gene from my family (and from two of my own past lives; my lifetime as *"le salaud de Paris,"* and my lifetime as a textile baron and "man of the world" in Genoa, Italy), I also inherited what I also refer to as my "ignorance" gene from my superstitious Roman Catholic family tree; which was why I was born with an insatiable hunger to know that compelled me to become a voracious reader at an early age.

Gurdjieff Was Wrong But His Teaching Works

At fifteen I acquired the encyclopedic set of books that I saw advertised in a magazine called *The Great Books of the Western World*; and in high school I discovered literature, and Ernest Hemingway became my romantic hero and literary mentor whose life I explored in my literary memoir *The Lion that Swallowed Hemingway*. But a lot of water had to flow under the bridge before I could write that book, which is the story of how I got to find the path in Gurdjieff's teaching while studying philosophy at university that saved me from myself.

I wanted to be a writer, but I was called to become a seeker with Somerset Maugham's novel *The Razor's Edge*; and despite how I tried to not heed the call, I kept getting pulled in the direction I was meant to go. I had a number of part-time jobs in high school, and after high school I worked at Camp 81 for Domtar cutting pulpwood with my Pioneer 620 chain saw first and then operating a Timberjack skidder, and I also worked in the Domtar paper mill in Red Rock on the shores of Lake Superior twelve miles from my hometown of Nipigon; but then synchronicity provided me with the opportunity to operate the local pool hall business in Nipigon, which I added to by including pin ball and vending machines, and I was making money well enough to expand and grow in the business world, but two years into the business and I got severed from my life by a sexual experience after work one night that shocked my conscience awake, and I sold my investment and went to Annecy, France where an Italian friend who worked in one of the bush camps had a sister and brother.

I took an ocean liner from New York City and sailed to Naples, Italy; and from Naples I took a bus to Paris, and from Paris I took a train to Annecy, in the *Haute-Savoie* region of France bordering Switzerland. And not more than a month of living in Annecy and I had an experience while practicing meditation one evening that accidentally opened up the chakra at the base of my spine and set free the Kundalini energy, known as the "serpent fire."

I felt the uncoiled "serpent" crawl up the canal of my spine and lodge itself into my brain, and it set my mind on fire. I recorded my experience on the blank pages of the front and back covers of my paperback copy of Emily Bronte's novel *Wuthering Heights* that I was reading at the time; and I'm glad I have a record of my Kundalini awakening to prove that it actually happened. It's dated *October 21, 1968*. I was twenty-three years old, very naïve, culturally shocked, and still reeling from my sexual experience; and this is what I wrote:

> *Tonight I think I have experienced meditation in its truest form. How and why I will explain. I had been reading a book,* Concentration: An Approach to Meditation; *and in it I read that to meditate one must so to speak become harmonious with what he is meditating on. The example it gave was a flower. It said to observe the flower very carefully the next time you passed a flower. To stop, pick up the flower, observe it, feel it, smell it, note its colors, its texture, everything about the flower, and then when you want to meditate, in your moment of tranquility to pick that beautiful little flower as your object of meditation.*
>
> *Well, I did this; only with a leaf. By sheer accident yesterday when I was waiting for the kids to come out of school I happened to pick up a fallen maple leaf. I fiddled around with it for a while, and then what I had read about the flower came to me, and I observed the leaf as closely as I could. I noted its color, its texture, its size, shape, and even its odor, and the conclusion I came to was that it was beautiful. It really was beautiful. I did not want to throw it away. I wanted to keep it forever and forever. I wanted it. I cherished it. I loved it. I loved a leaf! But then I thought of the absurdity of it all, and still I clung to it.*
>
> *I did not want to throw it away, and I did not until the young girls came out of school, for it was then that being forced by the sheer reality of our difference, because as I gave Sabrina and Patricia a kiss on the cheek I let it slip hesitantly from my hand and quickly grasped the girls' hands, one on each side, to get in touch with real people, real existence, and yet I could not stop feeling that that beautiful little leaf did have an existence of its own and that I had come to realize it. Now I believe it has. Here is what happened:*
>
> *I was sitting alone reading, and it was very quiet except for the ticking of a clock. Then the idea struck me to try meditation on that leaf I had so perspicaciously observed. I must note here that when I observed the leaf it was smooth and waxy on one side and the other was not so smooth owing to the veins which projected from the main stem to all the extremities of the leaf. And the stem was fine and*

thin on its attachment but thickened progressively as it neared its creator, and when the wind had separated it how there remained a slight yet noticeable hole which I made a note of recollecting at the time because if ever I was to meditate on that leaf my existence would become harmonious with its existence via this golden gate, and so I assumed the position directed in the book to sit with my feet flat on the floor, my back as straight as comfort would allow, my hands resting on my knees, and my head straight and my eyes looking straight ahead, and slowly I began to meditate on the leaf.

I began my meditation by observing first its size, shape, and form, and I viewed it mentally from all angles, up, down, sideways, frontwards, backwards, and then I observed its color, texture, and odor; then all my observations were meditated upon simultaneously with a center of concentration upon the golden gate. I concentrated and concentrated, and as I did so I repeated such lines to myself: "How beautiful you are. I want to be you. I want my existence to be your existence. I want that we should be one and the same. We will be harmonious." And as I repeated these lines I pictured my "self," my existence (and it was not normal, for I pictured my existence as shapeless, formless, without creation, as though it was the "me" of me) enter the golden gate slowly, very slowly, and as I began to enter my back began to stiffen, and the deeper my existence went into the existence of the leaf the more rigid my back became and the lighter my head felt, and the lighter it felt the more it began to float, and as the "me" of me entered into the veins of the leaf I felt a certain physical levitation which was climaxed by a certain mental euphoria as the "me" of me touched every extremity of the leaf and became one and the same as the "it" of it.

I consciously felt, for I had not by any means lost my powers of reason for I was still conscious of what was going on because deep down somewhere I knew it was just an experiment, but nevertheless I consciously felt a symbiosis, a union with the "me" and the "it" united to make "one". This had such a physical effect on me that the stiffening of my back and the weightlessness of my head, as though it wanted to leave the body and float away somewhere, snapped me into, so to speak, the materialistic reality of it all that it sent a momentary chill through me and in order for me to get back into the swing of things I decided to relinquish the experiment, but I did this carefully also.

I slowly withdrew my existence—the "me" from the "it" via the same means of entry, and curiously enough as I did this my back began to lose the rigidity it experienced and my head the weightlessness, and the further the "me" withdrew the more normal I became until when the "me" was completely removed and inharmonious with the "it" I felt the way I had begun my meditation, tranquil, phlegmatic, yet somehow thwarted.

It took the better part of ten years to harness the "serpent fire" of the Kundalini, which could have driven me out of my mind again like it did in my Sufi lifetime in medieval Persia had I not been hell-bent on finding my true self; but while in Annecy it got away on me and I fell into the seductive fantasy world of "automatic" writing shortly after playing around with a Ouija board one evening with my Italian friend's sister and her husband. But I managed to write my first novel while living in Annecy, inspired by Macbeth's famous soliloquy "Tomorrow, and tomorrow, and tomorrow creeps in this petty pace…"

When I returned to Canada and my hometown of Nipigon I burned the only copy of my novel *This Petty Pace* in an effort to detach myself from the fantasy world of my own confused mind, but not until I discovered Gurdjieff at university and began "working" on myself with his techniques of *self-remembering, non-identifying, conscious labor, intentional suffering,* and *non-considering* did I begin to harness the "serpent" of my undisciplined mind.

But in my second year at university, where I was called to study philosophy to continue my quest for my true self, I had the remarkable experience of witnessing my unconscious manifest a symbolic archetypal mandala before my eyes late one night after I gave up on trying to make sense of Gurdjieff's teaching.

I had read Ouspensky's book *In Search of the Miraculous* once already, and I was going through it again trying to penetrate the secret of how to "work" on myself, but I just couldn't "get it," and in frustration I threw the book onto my desk and flung myself on my bed to calm myself. I lay for a few minutes with my hands behind my head, and then I got up and shut the light and lay down again.

Gurdjieff Was Wrong But His Teaching Works

Gurdjieff frustrated the hell out of me, not because I couldn't "get" his teaching of "work on oneself," but because I knew with my whole being that his teaching was what I needed to find my *true self*; I just knew this.

As much as I loved philosophy, it wasn't taking me where I had to go to find the answer to the question that came to me one night in Annecy, France—the question that went to the very core of my *non-being* and had the power to motivate me to go to university to study philosophy to find the answer that would save me.

In a dream that night in Annecy, I left my body and entered into the mind of every single person in the world; and I took every question that every person had ever asked and reduced them all to one question: WHY AM I?

I didn't know it then, but that's the question that Noman asks; because no matter how much we grow in the consciousness of our *non-being,* we never know why we are, and my unconscious worked out the dilemma of our *false self* into a dream to inspire and motivate me to study philosophy to find the *raison d'être* of our *non-being*.

So there I was, laying on my bed in my second year of philosophy studies at Lakehead University stuck between the proverbial rock and hard place because philosophy was slowly casting me adrift in an open sea of endless speculation and Gurdjieff's teaching which I knew would save me wouldn't open up to me, and I stewed in my frustration—*and that's when the miracle happened!*

In the pitch dark of my bedroom a tiny dot of blue light appeared at the foot of my bed, just above my eye level. Startled, I stared at the dot wondering what it was; but as I stared the tiny dot of blue light began to expand before my eyes and formed a perfect donut-shaped circle about three feet in diameter.

Nonplussed, I stared and stared; and then a tiny dot of yellow light appeared within the circumference of the blue circle, at the top; and it rested there for a moment or so before it expanded into a straight line within the circumference and stopped; and then it made a ninety degree turn and formed another straight line and stopped; and then it made another ninety degree turn and formed a third straight line, and then a fourth straight line that connected with itself at the top to make a perfect square of yellow light within the circle of blue light!

I stared at the symbolically "squared circle" for what seemed like forever, and then it disappeared before my eyes and I stared into the darkness like nothing had happened; and it took many years before I learned from C. G. Jung that my own unconscious had responded to my dilemma by manifesting the archetypal symbol of the whole Self in the "squared circle" mandala to give me the assurance that I would need to find my *true self* and return the "fish's scale" back to God where my lost soul belonged; and, if my memory serves me (which I can't really trust), that weekend I drove home to Nipigon and went on my walk where I created my *Royal Dictum* that opened up Gurdjieff's teaching and changed my life forever…

6. Roses/Thorns

"First roses roses, then thorns thorns," said Gurdjieff; and that's the path that I embarked upon with my *Royal Dictum*...

I couldn't "get" Gurdjieff's teaching of "work on oneself," because this path of self-transformation cannot be apprehended by the mind; it can only be apprehended by personal experience. And until one "does" the teaching, one will always be on the outside looking in; that's why my unconscious inspired my *Royal Dictum*—because this was my entry point into Gurdjieff's teaching of conscious, intentional self-transformation.

"Fusion, inner unity, is obtained by means of 'friction,' by the struggle between 'yes' and 'no' in man," said Gurdjieff in one of his talks that Ouspensky recorded in his book *In Search of the Miraculous*; and this spoke to me personally, because I had to find a way out of the fantasy world of my own very confused mind.

"In what way can one evoke this struggle between 'yes' and 'no' in oneself?" Gurdjieff was asked in the same talk; and his reply confirmed the "inspired" logic of my *Royal Dictum*: "Sacrifice is necessary," said Gurdjieff. "If nothing is sacrificed nothing is obtained. And it is necessary to sacrifice something precious at the moment, to sacrifice for a long time and to sacrifice a great deal. *But still, not forever.* This must be understood because often it is not understood. Sacrifice is necessary only when the process of crystallization is going on. When crystallization is achieved, renunciations, privations, and sacrifices are no longer necessary. Then a man may have everything he wants. There are no longer any laws for him, he is a law unto himself' (*In Search of the Miraculous*, P. D. Ouspensky, p. 33).

With 20/20 hindsight, this makes perfect sense to me now; but not at the time, because I had vowed to live my *Royal Dictum* for the rest of my life and I was going into my future "blind" not unlike King Oedipus. But as Gurdjieff said, I didn't have to live by my edict of self-denial for the rest of my life once it had served its purpose, which miraculously happened only three and a half years later; and I dropped my *Royal Dictum* and got on with my life as though I had just left a monastic order and gone back into the world of desire and pleasure, but I will tell this part of my story later when I have more context. Imagine then the turmoil of inner conflict of 'yes' and 'no' that I unleased upon myself that day when I stepped off the breakwater and onto the mainland with my *Royal Dictum* to guide me…

This is a part of my story that I don't want to tell, but in the interest of full disclosure I have to tell it because it speaks to the salvific factor of Gurdjieff's teaching that liberated me from the seductive hold my mind had upon me; and it all started with my Kundalini experience and that damn Ouija board back in Annecy, France when I opened myself up to negative psychic influences.

How or why I started this dangerous habit, I can only attribute to my desperate loneliness and mental confusion; but after my Ouija board experience I began to toy with the idea of making contact with psychic entities through "automatic" writing.

I asked a question on paper and waited for my hand to respond, and gradually I began to get answers to all my questions; but never, never was I able to confirm that the answers I got came from anything other than my own mind; but despite the absence of any objective confirmation, "automatic" writing was seductive because it temporarily satisfied my voracious appetite for egoic gratification.

And then it became dangerous, because my egoic desires pulled me in deeper and deeper into the fantasy scenarios that I created in my mind, like a novelist who gets involved with the characters he has brought to life in his imaginary story.

I no longer needed pen and paper to conjure up my scenarios, I began to talk to the "psychic" entities in my mind; and when I was alone, I did so out loud. But when I was in public I made sure that my mental conversations were silent.

Eight or nine years after I overcame this dangerous mental habit, which I did by relentlessly sublimating my Kundalini energy into my contract painting business, creative writing, and long distance running, I noticed a young man in my hometown who was afflicted with the same treacherous mental habit; but no one noticed but me.

Gurdjieff Was Wrong But His Teaching Works

His lips did not move when he talked to himself, even among friends over drinks in one of the local bars, but I knew he was talking with the "entities" in his own mind; and one day I saw him standing in the rain outside the Nipigon Café talking to himself, and I pulled over and said, "Get in the car, Mark!"

He looked at me, confused; but I insisted, and he got in out of the rain and I drove down Highway Eleven to Five Mile Park where I went for my daily run, and I told him that I knew what he was doing and that he needed professional help.

"I've been where you are, Mark; and it's a very dangerous place to be," I said to him, after convincing him that he wasn't fooling anyone but himself. "And if you don't get professional help, you're going to destroy your life."

And sure enough, several weeks later they found his body in a hotel room. He had overdosed on drugs and left a wife and young family behind; but he could have saved himself had he gone for professional help for his obsessive introversion.

I didn't go for professional help, because I didn't want to be stigmatized with a psychiatric record, which I know now was foolish; instead, I found Gurdjieff at university whose teaching of the many selves offered me the solution to my problem.

"Man has no individuality. He has no single, big I. Man is divided into a multiplicity of small I's…*Man is a plurality.* Man's name is legion," said Gurdjieff; and he promised that by "work on oneself" I could fuse the many I's of my fragmented ego into a single individual self. That's what attracted me to Gurdjieff's teaching from the outset, which I initiated myself into with my edict of self-denial that I called my *Royal Dictum*; and by "working" on myself I integrated and fused the many I's of my fragmented ego personality, and I saved myself...

It would be fitting now to reveal that in all the years that I lived Gurdjieff's teaching, and even after all these many years later, I never once belonged to a Gurdjieff group let alone met another student of Gurdjieff's teaching, save in my dreams (my philosophy professors at university had not even heard of Gurdjieff or his Fourth Way teaching); and all the wisdom that I garnered from his teaching came from reading everything I could get on Gurdjieff and his teaching and my relentless efforts in *self-remembering, non-identifying, conscious labor, intentional suffering,* and especially *non-considering*—Gurdjieff's fundamental techniques for fusing and uniting the fragmented consciousness of one's many I's and "creating" a central I that one could justly call his true, individual self.

But what motivated me to go to such impossible extremes? Whatever possessed me to say to God that I would pay whatever was asked of me to find my true self? Where did my inspiration come from to "square the circle" and "create" my own immortal soul? This is the heart of my story, and the only way I can reveal how I found my lost soul would be to talk about my personal *daemon*, the driving spirit of my personal destiny.

In *The Soul's Code, In Search of Character and Calling*, the noted Jungian analyst James Hillman wrote: "The soul of each of us is given a unique *daemon* before we are born, and it has selected an image or pattern that we live on earth. This soul-companion, the *daemon,* guides us here; in the process of arrival, however, we forget all that took place and believe we come empty into this world. The *daemon* remembers what is in your image and belongs to your pattern, and therefore your *daemon* is the carrier of your destiny" (*The Soul's Code, In Search of Character and Calling*, James Hillman, p. 8).

Hillman calls this individual destiny "the acorn theory." Like the acorn seed that *has* to become an oak tree because that is the acorn seed's pattern, so too are we destined to become who we are meant to be because of our personal *daemon.*

"There was a *daemon* in me, and in the end its presence proved to be decisive," wrote Carl Jung in *Memories, Dreams, Reflections.* "It overpowered me, and if I was at times ruthless it was because I was in the grip of my *daemon.* I could never stop at anything once attained. I had to hasten on, to catch up with my vision. Since my contemporaries, understandably, could not perceive my vision, they saw only a fool rushing ahead, (but) I had to obey an inner law which was imposed upon me and left me no freedom of choice," Jung explained; and so was I driven by my own relentless *daemon.*

How many times in my life I was called a fool for rushing into something that defied reason, I cannot say—like leaving my thriving pool hall and vending machine business and going to France; dropping out of university in my third year with no plausible explanation; starting my own house-painting business with next-to-no experience and finances; building my triplex with only nineteen dollars in my bank account, a paucity of carpentry skills and hardly any tools; exploring an offshoot Christian solar cult teaching that did irreparable damage to my eyesight; and self-publishing two novel memoirs that shocked the shadow personality of my hometown of Nipigon and forced Penny and I to relocate to Georgian Bay, South central Ontario for peace of mind; that's why I kept my inner work with Gurdjieff's teaching, my *Royal Dictum*, and the sayings of Jesus to myself; because no one would have understood my *daemonic* imperative to find my *true self*. To anyone who knew me, I defied the logic of rational behavior, and they labelled me strange, odd, and even crazy.

Be that as it may, as much respect as I have for Hillman's "acorn theory," which I believe to be essentially true and which Hillman supports with anecdotal evidence of people that were called to their destiny, it makes infinitely more sense to me within the expanded paradigm of karma and reincarnation because of my past-life regressions that allowed me to personally experienc**e the original archetypal pattern of the hero's journey.**

If I may explain. The three stages of the hero's journey, according to Joseph Campbell's *The Hero with a Thousand Faces*, are 1, SEPARATION; 2, INITIATION; and 3, the RETURN. In one of my regressions I experienced myself as an atom of God in the Body of God, and I was SEPARATED from God when I was sent into the Earth world; and I was INITATED into the evolutionary process of life to take in the vital life force, which is the *"I Am"* consciousness of Soul, until I had constellated enough life force to give birth to a new "I" of God, which I did in my first primordial human lifetime; and I continued to evolve in the consciousness of my individual self through the natural process of karma and reincarnation until I had realized enough self-consciousness to take evolution into my own hands and break the cycle of karma and reincarnation with Gurdjieff's teaching, my *Royal Dictum,* and the sayings of Jesus and give birth to my spiritual self in my mother's kitchen while she was kneading bread dough on the kitchen table that day—or, as Gurdjieff believed, until I "created" my own immortal soul; and I RETURNED back home to God where I came from, which my unconscious foretold with my poem *Noman* in high school and confirmed with the symbolic "squaring of the circle" in my second year of philosophy studies at Lakehead University in Thunder Bay.

    I *lived* and *fulfilled* the archetypal hero's journey, then; this is why I can confidentially say that Gurdjieff was wrong in his premise that man is not born with an immortal soul, but correct in the execution of his teaching…

7. The Way of Soul

Carl Jung's inner self anguished under the oppressive burden of his successful outer self, and he cried out: "My soul, where are you? Do you hear me? I speak. I call you—are you there? I have returned, I am here again. I have shaken the dust of all the lands from my feet, and I have come to you, I am with you. After long years of long wandering, I have come to you again. Should I tell you everything I have seen, experienced, and drunk in? Or do you not want to hear about all the noise of life and the world? But one thing you must know: the one thing that I have learned is that one must live this life. *This life is the way, the long sought-after way to the unfathomable, which we call divine. There is no other way, all other ways are false paths*" (*The Red Book*, A Reader's Edition, pages 127-8, Italics mine).

This is why Carl Gustav Jung became my personal hero, because he initiated himself into the secret way of life and became a *knower*...

When I learned that Amazon was offering *The Red Book*, A Reader's Edition, for under thirty dollars (the original large illustrated copy that came out two years earlier was just under two hundred dollars, which my budget would not allow for since my open heart operation that effectively ended my working life as a drywall taper and house painter) I put it on my Amazon Wish List, and Penny bought it for me, along with half a dozen other books, for my Christmas gift; but it was shipped separately from my other books and didn't arrive until several days after Christmas.

On Friday, *December 28, 2012*, at *11: 50 A. M.*, while listening to a lecture online by Stephen A. Hoeller on "Gnosticism: A New Light on the Ancient Tradition of Inner Knowing," CANPAR delivered my copy of *The Red Book* right to my front door. I opened it excitedly and began reading; and I finished reading the 600 hundred page tome at *8: 35 A. M., January 1, 2013*, barely five days later, after just listening to Hoeller's online lecture "Christ: the Misunderstood

Redeemer," and I can honestly say that *The Red Book* was the most engrossing read of my entire life, despite the strain that it put on my impaired eyesight!

I understood now why Jung could not risk his career by publishing *The Red Book* during his lifetime, which he later wisely called an exercise in "active imagination." His sanity would have been seriously questioned (as mine would have had I disclosed my obsession with "automatic" writing); so he put it away and fifty years later his family gave permission for Jungian scholar/historian Sonu Shamdasani, who wrote the introduction to *The Red Book*, to prepare Jung's chronicle of his "confrontation with the unconscious" and release it to an eagerly waiting public; and it was worth the wait.

The way that Jung brought closure to *The Red Book* brought tears to my eyes, because it spoke the divine mystery of human suffering (which I demystified in my memoir *The Pearl of Great Price*) that has puzzled the world ever since Jesus sacrificed his life upon the cross to impress upon the world the symbolic power of his teaching of "dying" to one's life to "save" one's life. "It was noon on a hot summer's day and I was taking a stroll in my garden; when I reached the shade of the high trees, I met Philemon strolling in the fragrant grass. But when I sought to approach him, a blue shade came from the other side, and when Philemon saw him, he said, 'I find you in the garden, beloved. The sins of the world have conferred beauty upon your countenance,'" wrote Jung in *The Red Book,* as he brings closure to his heroic quest for his lost soul.

Philemon is Jung's "inner guru"—which later in life Jung wisely called his "superior insight" and which in the teachings of the Way of the Eternal that I lived for over thirty years after Gurdjieff's teaching calls the "Inner Master" and Ralph Waldo Emerson called the "Oversoul" and "God within" and today I simply refer to as my Higher Self, my Muse, and also the omniscient guiding force of life—and Philemon and the blue shade, which is identified as Jesus Christ in Jung's chronicle, talk about "the worm."

And then Philemon says: "I know only one thing, that whoever hosts the worm also needs his brother. What do you bring, my beautiful guest? Lamentation and abomination were the gift of the worm. What will you give us?

"The shade (Jesus) answered, 'I bring you the beauty of suffering. That is what is needed by whoever hosts the worm.'"

This ends *The Red Book*, with Jesus implying that suffering kills the worm.

Very few people will pierce the secret of the transformative power of the Holy Flame of God in human suffering, which is why Jesus called it "the beauty of suffering," but human suffering is beautiful because through suffering we grow in the consciousness of our divine nature; and this speaks to the *intentional suffering* of Gurdjieff's teaching, my *Royal Dictum*, and the sayings of Jesus that I incorporated into the path that I was forging for myself out of my own humble life as a house painter in Nipigon, Ontario and which awakened me to the secret way that Jung alluded to in his commentary to *The Secret of the Golden Flower*.

The secret way of life is not a secret at all, because it is life itself; but not until one has "eyes" to see and "ears" to hear will one recognize that life itself is the Way; and it takes a long time and much life experience to grow enough in consciousness to become aware of the secret way of life. This is what made Gurdjieff's teaching so effective; because "work on oneself" sped up the life process and awakened one to the secret way!

Despite all the thought that I have given in my efforts to explain the secret way—which in one way or another every one of my books has addressed—I still have difficulty conceptualizing the principle of inherent self-transcendence that is central to the secret way of life, but unless I make this clear there will be no point in continuing with my story; and so I implore my Muse to assist me. But is my Muse a metaphor for superior insight, or am I being literal in my invocation?

Both. When I implore my Muse I implore my Higher Self, which would be the deepest thought that I am capable of; but in my invocation I seek to go beyond myself and connect with the creative principle of life, which has just popped that haunting existential question into my mind best expressed by the Preacher in *Ecclesiastes*: **"What profit hath a man of all his labour which he taketh under the sun?"** Because in the answer to this question lies the mystery of our existence.

In his quest for his lost soul, Jung had to take the plunge and go deep into himself (which he called his "confrontation with the unconscious") to look for that part of himself that he had forfeited to achieve his worldly goals; and in the process he learned the most valuable lesson of any seeker's life—that *"this life is the way, the long sought-after way to the unfathomable, which we call divine."* That's the truth that Gurdjieff taught me with his teaching of "work on oneself," because the more I transformed the consciousness of my *non-being* (my shadow self) by "working" on myself, the more the secret way of life answered the Preacher's haunting question **"What profit hath a man of all his labour which he taketh under the sun?"**

Our life is not "a useless passion" as Sartre contended with his philosophy of *being* and *non-being*; because everything that we do in life nourishes what Jung called the "process of individuation," which makes man far from being a useless passion. But not until we understand what is meant by the "process of individuation" will we ferret out the secret way of life; and this is what my story is all about.

So if life is not a "useless passion" and all of our energies are automatically poured into the individuation of our own *becoming*, then what is the point of it all? That's what the Preacher wanted to know with his haunting question, which I finally managed to answer with the quest for my own lost soul; because when I found my true self all the pieces of the puzzle fell into place and I finally caught sight of the big picture.

"There is a doctrine uttered in secret that man is a prisoner who has no right to open the door of his prison and run away; this is a great mystery which I do not quite understand," said Socrates in Plato's *Phaedo*; but Socrates was being ironic, as was his nature, because he not only understood the mystery but provided us with the key to our prison door with his philosophy of self-transcendence. But what is our prison? And is it really a prison, or is it the *I Am Principle of Life* unfolding through natural evolution?

Our life is our prison, said Socrates; and death is the key to our prison door. "I deem that the true disciple of philosophy is likely to be misunderstood by other men; they do not perceive that he is ever pursuing death and dying," said Socrates in the *Phaedo*; and by "death" he meant "the habit of the soul gathering and collecting into herself." This is the mystery of **conscious individuation**, because by "habit" Socrates meant the art of separating one's inner self from one's outer self until one *becomes* one's Higher Self. This is what I discovered with my *Royal Dictum*, which awakened me to the secret way of life…

There is so much confusion about the self that it is next to impossible to see the simplicity of our true nature. "Vanity of vanities, all is vanity," said the Preacher; but in the end he came to see that life is meant for living, because in the living man *becomes* who he is meant to be, which removes the hollow sting of vanity.

"Of making many books there is no end," said the Preacher, "and much study is a weariness of the flesh. Let us hear the conclusion of the whole matter: Fear God, and keep his commandments; for this is the whole duty of man. For God will bring every work into judgment, with every secret thing, whether it be good, or whether it be evil." But why? What is the judgment of God?

The Preacher tells us to obey the commandments of God, because whatever we do will be brought into judgement one day; and not until we understand what the Preacher meant by this judgment will we see the big picture. And that's precisely what my infernal *daemon* revealed to me in high school with my symbolic poem *Noman*.

I was called to judgment by God in my poem, and I was found wanting. God wanted a reckoning for the life he had granted me, but I could not give him what he wanted because I did not have it. God wanted his "fish's scale," and he banished me back into the world to look for my lost soul which was not mine but his; and not until I found my lost soul and returned it to God would God allow me back into his kingdom.

It was all there, in my high school poem *Noman*, and so powerful was Noman's imperative to find his lost soul that I had no choice but to become a seeker; and when our English teacher assigned Somerset Maugham's novel *The Razor's Edge* for us to read, I heard the call of Soul like Maugham's hero Larry Darrel and my fate was sealed—but my God, it took a long time to make sense out of my confused life!

This is the time to say something about myself that I never understood but which drove me to despair so many times that I ended up calling life an old whore that loved to screw me of my virtue, which many years later I wrote about in *Old Whore Life, Exploring the Shadow Side of Karma*, a book of spiritual musings that I posted on my blog first and later self- published and sold on Amazon; a book that I can trace back to my high school poem *Noman* and that critical time in my life when I had to confront my unconscious and plunge into the depths of my personal and family shadow to find my lost soul, out of which was born my most personal and terrifying saying—*the shortest way to God is through hell!*

So as allegorical as my poem *Noman* was, it was no less personal; because I had to work my way through my own karma both past and present to find my lost soul, which I'm happy to say I did. This is why I can speak with gnostic certainty about my quest for my lost soul, and why I *know* that Gurdjieff was wrong in his premise that man is not born with an immortal soul but correct in the execution of his teaching; because without his teaching I would not have found my true self that was lost in the *non-being* of my shadow.

But how could Gurdjieff be so wrong and so right about man's immortal soul? Whatever possessed him to believe that we have to create our own soul? This is the mystery of *enantiodromia* and essential truth of my strange story; and now I must jump in and get to the nitty-gritty of my **conscious individuation**, however incredible and strange the story of my own *becoming* may seem to be...

The Preacher in *Ecclesiastes* was a wise man, and he brought us right up to the gates of the kingdom of heaven (our true self); but he did not provide us with the key to enter, just as my hero C. G. Jung, a man no less wise than the Preacher, brought us to the gates of the kingdom but could not provide us with the key either. The most that Jung could do was to point us in the right direction. "What nature leaves imperfect, the art perfects," said Jung, quoting the ancient alchemists for validation; which simply means that nature will only evolve us so far and then we have to take evolution into our own hands to realize our full potential.

By "art" the alchemists meant the secret way, which Jung found and made central to his psychology in what he called the "process of individuation." But *"no one knows how the paradoxical wholeness of man can ever be realized. That is the crux of individuation,"* said C. G. Jung in Barbara Hannah's memoir, realizing the problem of man's *becoming*.

Both Jung and the Preacher initiated themselves into the secret way, but they could not solve the mystery of how to "make the two into one," as Jesus did; and this left them standing at the gates of the kingdom staring in wonder. That's why Jung came to me in a dream many years after I transcended myself that day in my mother's kitchen; he had to find the key to the kingdom of our true self.

Penny and I had only been living in Georgian Bay a few years when I began a literary experiment not unlike the exercise that Jung called "active imagination" just to sublimate all of that energy that I had set free with the explosion of consciousness that I had with seven past-life regressions, because after I wrote my novel *Cathedral of My Past Lives* I still had so much creative energy that I had to do something with it; and I dictated a series of "Soul talk" books into my mini tape recorder as I commuted to work each day.

I was working in Creemore that year, taping and painting, which was an hour's drive from our home in Bluewater, Georgian Bay; so I brought along my mini recorder which I hung on my rear view mirror and I talked my "Soul talks" books on my long drive to and from work each day; and the first book that came out of me I called *The Way of Soul*, which caught Carl Jung's attention and pulled him into my world in a dream one night.

I said that this was a strange story, but the truth is that this "Soul talk" book that caught Jung's attention even now six or seven years after I talked it into my recorder has not even been transcribed yet, let alone published; but apparently on the Other Side it was already published soon after I recorded it, and Jung came to me in a dream with my book *The Way of Soul* in his hand because he wanted to talk to me about the secret way of life.

We talked for what could have even been longer than his legendary talk of thirteen hours with Sigmund Freud when they first met in Vienna, but it didn't seem that long because it was a dream. On the Other Side time does not concur with time out here; and so moved was I by our conversation that I had to include Jung in my novel *The Waking Dream* that was inspired by an unbelievable experience that I had when I came home one Sunday morning from a long drive to Midhurst where I had gone to give a painting estimate for my work and from which I had just talked a whole chapter on the ontological nature of the ego self for my third "Soul talk" book, *The Soul of Happiness.*

I will relate this mind-blowing experience that inspired my novel *The Waking Dream* when I have provided more context, but for now suffice to say that the circumstances that brought the renowned co-founder of depth psychology into my life were inspired by my first "Soul talk" book *The Way of Soul,* because it offered a solution to Jung's dilemma of what in our dream conversation he called "the problem of the alpha and omega of the self."

Jung spent his whole life studying the human personality, but he could never fathom the deepest mystery of the self—where it came from, where it was going, and how it was going to get there. And how he got a copy of my book *The Way of Soul* I don't know, because it was a long way from being published out here in the physical world; but he did, and we talked about the natural way of Soul that I had discovered with the help of my *Royal Dictum*, Gurdjieff's teaching, and the sayings of Jesus.

What I had discovered about the alpha and omega of the self was the ancient truth that we do not have a soul, as such; but rather that we are Soul in the process of evolving an individual "I", which I had experienced with my past-life regression to the Body of God where I experienced myself as an atom of God without an "I" and then in my first primordial human lifetime where I had the dawning of my reflective self-consciousness which evolved from lifetime to lifetime until I was evolved enough to take evolution into my own hands in my current lifetime and consciously individuated myself, which I did with my *Royal Dictum*, Gurdjieff's teaching, and the sayings of Jesus.

And this resolved the mystery of Gurdjieff's belief that we are not born with an immortal soul but can "create" our own soul with *conscious effort* and *intentional suffering*, which I have called **conscious individuation.**

As difficult as it may be to believe, the simple truth is that we begin life on Earth as a spark of divine consciousness that John Keats called "atoms of perception" in a letter to his brother, and as we evolve through the many stages of life we take in the creative life force, which I experienced to be the *"I Am"* consciousness of Soul, and we grow in our Soul nature until we have acquired enough *"I Am"* consciousness for our Soul nature to become aware of itself for the first time, as I did in my primordial human lifetime as the alpha male of a group of ten or twelve higher primates when I experienced the birth of my own "I".

    This is how Gurdjieff could be both right and wrong about the immortal soul of man; we are *not* conscious of our immortal nature until we take evolution into our own hands and *become* conscious of our immortal nature, which Gurdjieff knew how to do with a remarkable teaching that he put together from various esoteric sources that he discovered in his long and arduous search for the meaning and purpose of life, an eclectic teaching of spiritual growth that he called "esoteric Christianity" because Jesus taught the same teaching but which in reality is a conscious understanding of the secret way of life that I finally came to recognize as the natural way of Soul that excited Jung's imagination and pulled him into my dream world, and the more we talked the more his excited little eyes twinkled; and this now provides me with the context that I need to explain the mystery of our *becoming…*

8. The Secret Way of Life

And so, the pivotal question to my strange story has to be: how did I become aware of the secret way of life? And just what is this secret way, anyway?

To answer this question I have to explain how I was driven by my *daemon* to find my true self, because to find my true self I had to search everywhere; which meant, unfortunately (or fortunately, because as Gurdjieff liked to say **"every stick has two ends"**), my search led me to some false spiritual teachings that took up much of my time, energy, and finances before I found them out. But that's the risk one has to take when one is destined to blaze their own trail, as I had to do; but my studies were not in vain, because from these false teachings I learned much about myself and the shadow side of life.

Because life *is* the way, as I came to learn as I "worked" on myself with Gurdjieff's teaching and which Jung confirmed many years later when I read the strange story of his own "confrontation with the unconscious" in *The Red Book*, it is everywhere to be found; but one has to see the logic of life's purpose to understand that life is the secret way to the kingdom of one's true self; and **the logic of life's purpose is to expand the consciousness of God through the evolution of Soul through life**.

Unfortunately, the only way to see the logic of life is to live the secret way; but one has to find it first, and the only way to find the secret way is to *live* it. This is the mystery of the secret way, because as one *lives* the secret way the secret way of life reveals itself. This is the paradoxical challenge of the secret way of life.

For example, Jesus said*: "He that loveth his life shall lose it; and he that hateth his life in this world shall keep it unto life eternal."* Logic would ask: how is it possible to find one's life by dying to one's life? That sounds like madness; but it's not madness at all, as I came to see when I "died" to my desires as I lived my *Royal Dictum,* which was my personal edict of self-denial that I vowed to live for the rest of my life in my quest for my true self.

Gurdjieff Was Wrong But His Teaching Works

My life in this world was my life of sensual desire; pleasures in sex, smoking, drinking, eating, personal self-image, and countless little pleasures that I wasn't even aware of until I became acutely conscious of my worldly life as I lived my *Royal Dictum*, and as I denied myself I "died" to these desires. But obviously this was not a physical death (though there were times when physical death would have been much easier), and it's this metaphorical death of our *non-being* self that Jesus referred to; but who would know this unless they lived the mystery of dying to one's life to find one's life?

Socrates knew, that's who. This is what he meant by "the habit of soul gathering and collecting herself into herself." And by "true disciple of philosophy" who is "ever pursuing death and dying," Socrates meant a *knower* of the secret way who consciously lives the philosophy of dying to one's live to find one's life; and by "philosophy" Socrates specifically meant this power that transforms the *non-being* consciousness of one's ego/shadow personality into the consciousness of one's transcendent self that is above one's *being* and *non-being* self. In short, one has to *become* one's true self to *be* one's true self; that's the paradoxical nature of the individuation process.

This is all very abstruse, but Socrates makes it clear that the true disciple of philosophy lives a life of virtue, because the virtuous life purifies one's consciousness of the vanity of one's *non-being* and renders the soul pure. *"And what is purification but the separation of the soul from the body, as I was saying before,"* said Socrates; *"the habit of the soul gathering and collecting herself into herself?"*

Logic would dictate then that as one *lives* a life of virtue (Socrates called Goodness the most noble of all the virtues, and most efficient), one will transcend himself; which means, as I eventually came to deduce, that there is an inherent power of self-transcendence in the noble virtues—*but only if one lives them!*

As simple as it may be, by *living* a life of virtue one activates this miraculous power and transforms the consciousness of one's *non-being* and realizes their true self; which is why when I discovered this Socratic dynamic of self-transcendence in his philosophy I created another ethic to live by along with my *Royal Dictum,* which I repeated every morning before I went to work each day: *I promise to be honest and fair in all that I say and do.* But believe me, this was not easy to live by, given that I was just starting out in my house-painting business which I knew very little about and had to pretend that I knew what I was doing just to get work to make a living. *Talk about putting myself through the ringer!*

I created my *Royal Dictum* in my second year of philosophy studies at LU in Thunder Bay, Ontario; and I dropped out of university in my third year, so I never obtained a degree. But I had no choice, really; I was cruelly severed from my life once again by the ineluctable forces of my *daemonic* fate; and I got a job in one of the bush camps for Great Lakes north of Thunder Bay as a skidder operator, because I had experience working as a skidder operator in my youth for Nipigon Woodlands at Camp 81 not far from my hometown of Nipigon.

At this point in my story I have to relate a strange experience that I had with my mother that took me many years to unravel which speaks to the psychic dynamic of life, an experience that went a long way to helping me pierce the mystery of man's primordial survival instinct which became central to my understanding of what Gurdjieff called "the way of the sly man."

This is such an elusive mystery that I have to take time out to explain it as I relate the experience with my mother that woke me up to the exchange of psychic energies between people. This mystery is central to Gurdjieff's teaching, because it gives one a better understanding of **conscious individuation**. In short, it will help to understand why one has to "work" on oneself to grow into the person they are meant to be.

But the strange thing about this experience with my mother is that I can trace this exchange of psychic energies right back to my first primordial human lifetime that I experienced in my past life regression when I gave birth to my reflective self; and it has to do with the psychic energy that we need to grow in our own identity, because in that lifetime I was the alpha male and I appropriated the vital life force of my clan's will-to-be by keeping them all in a state of fear and submission. In fact, I wrote a short story to convey how this exchange of psychic energies is played out today in a family dynamic; a story that I called "Needs and Creature Comforts," for my book *Enantiodromia and Other Stories*.

Gurdjieff Was Wrong But His Teaching Works

In my story, Donny Stewart lords it over his wife and children, which is how he feeds his rapacious ego/shadow personality and grows in self-identity. But because he robs his wife and children of their will-to-be by brute force ("Do what I tell you, or else—") he creates karma that obligates him to pay his wife and children back for the psychic energy that he steals from them by forcing them to forfeit their will-to-be to him. This binds him to the recurring cycle of life and death until he has evolved enough to see how karma works and learns to become a GIVER instead of a TAKER, which is necessary to realize his wholeness and fulfill his destiny, as I had to do. This is what makes my story strange.

Everything that lives needs energy to grow, and so does the self. The self is not born fully realized, whole and complete as it were; it comes into the world as a spark of divine consciousness; an "atom of perception" as Keats perceived and I experienced, a soul seed that is encoded to evolve through life to realize its divine nature, which it does when it gives birth to a reflective self-consciousness that evolves through the natural process of karma and reincarnation until it has grown enough to take evolution into its own hands, as every person must do to become who they are meant to be because this is man's destiny.

Man has to take evolution into his own hands eventually, because the natural process of growth through karma and reincarnation cannot generate the special kind of energy (which I came to call "virtue") that one needs to transcend oneself and break the recurring cycle of life and death; that can only be done through **conscious individuation.** This is why people that have evolved as far as nature can take them suffer as they do, because life can no longer satisfy the longing in their soul for wholeness and completeness; and they despair from one lifetime to the next until they find the secret way and master the art of **conscious individuation**, as I managed to do in my current lifetime with Gurdjieff's teaching.

Now I can relate the experience that I had with my mother that awakened me to the exchange of psychic energies that people need to grow in self-identity. When I dropped out of university in my third year, I felt compelled by my *daemon* to leave; I heard the call, and I had to go out into the world to find my true self, because university had done all it could for me and my fate beckoned.

I had no idea what I was going to do, but I had to do something. I knew I had to stay at home for my mother's sake because of my father's drinking and unpredictable behavior, which I may explain later in my story; but I was so vulnerable the day I told my mother that I had just dropped out of university that I opened myself up to the experience that awakened me to man's primordial survival instinct of feeding off other people's psychic energies.

My mother and I were sitting in the living room. We were sitting in separate chairs, about two or three feet apart. I don't remember where my father was, or what he was doing; but I remember how vulnerable I felt, and the memory still makes me shudder. I told my mother that I had just quit university and was going to look for a job, my voice breaking with emotion; but within seconds I felt the strangest sensation of my energy being sucked out of me and flowing directly into my mother, in what seemed to be her solar plexus region.

I knew that my mother wasn't doing this consciously, it was purely instinctive; but the more my energy left my body, the more power I felt my mother had over me. And that's when I learned to never again show my mother or anybody else my vulnerability, no matter what the circumstances; because in my loss of energy to my mother I realized that it's to man's primordial nature to feed off another's psychic energies, and I had to learn to protect myself from what I later came to call Old Whore Life who loves to screw us of our "virtue"—exactly the same kind of experience that Gurdjieff had after his motor vehicle accident when he was convalescing at the Priory (his Institute for the Harmonious Development of Man) and felt his life force sucked out of him by some of his students, which led to his decision to close the Institute and initiate another form of teaching the Fourth Way.

That's how I learned to live "the way of the sly man," which over time awakened me to the shadow side of our personality that lives off the psychic energies of other people; a purely instinctive habit that most people aren't aware of but which is responsible for the contention and strife in relationships that our ego/shadow personality needs to grow in the consciousness of its *non-being* that keeps us trapped in life's prison.

But I didn't love my mother any less for instinctively sucking the vital life force out of me when I was so emotionally vulnerable; I simply became aware of the shadow side of her personality, and my father's too, which was more dangerous than my mother's because of his drinking; but I don't want to go there yet. I need more context to tell that part of my story.

I loved my parents, but I was waking up to my family's archetypal shadow that went back centuries; and thank God I discovered C. G. Jung in my quest for my true self, because his psychology spared me the grief that comes with blind spiritual ignorance. As St. Padre Pio said to me in one of my spiritual healing sessions which I wrote about in my novel *Healing with Padre Pio*, **"understanding heals the soul,"** and the more I studied Jung, the more I broke the hold that my Roman Catholic belief in evil had over me, because Jung saw our shadow as the dark side of our personality and the devil as the collective shadow of humanity. In the words of the mystic poet Rumi, "If thou hast not seen the devil, look at thine own self."

There's so much more to the story of my relationship with my parents that I don't know where to begin, but for now suffice to say that my mother believed in *malocchio,* which is Italian for the evil eye; and she could do a secret prayer ritual to dispel *"la fascino* (spell) which was an ancient folk ritual that broke the psychic hold of *malocchio.*

This is difficult to explain, but I know it's true because I experienced it many times growing up in our family home; but I have to explain how it works because it speaks to the mysterious psychic vampirism that goes on between people, and it will provide the context that I need to explain the mysterious "way of the sly man" as I lived it.

Let me illustrate this with a typical scenario taken straight out of our family home, one which would happen four or five times a month, especially with an older brother and one of my sisters. They would come home feeling sapped of all their energy, and they yawned and yawned as they frantically took in the vital life force that's in the air we breathe to replenish the psychic energy that was being drained out of them by the evil eye that someone had given them; and then they would ask Mom to do *la fascino* for them to cast out the evil eye.

Mom would ask for my brother's handkerchief, or something that he wore that day; and she would hold it in her hand and say her silent secret prayers that dispelled the evil eye, and we knew that it was working when my mother started to yawn. And the frequency and intensity of her yawns depended upon how strong a hold *malocchio* had over my siblings; meaning, the stronger the spell the more my mother yawned to replenish the vital life force that was being psychically drained from my brother or sister.

Sometimes *malocchio* was so strong that my siblings would feel nauseous, or have a splitting headache; and I know this to be true because Mom did *la fascino* for me many times over the years. In fact, so fascinated was I by *la fascino* that I asked my mother to teach me the secret prayer ritual one Christmas Eve, which apparently was the only time that one could pass on the sacred prayers that broke the spell of *malocchio;* and although I have an entirely different take on this ancient folk ritual for breaking the spell of the evil eye, I've healed Penny many times when she came home from work zapped of her vital life force, and it all has to do with the subtle exchange of psychic energies between people.

Because it's a secret tradition, I cannot reveal the sacred prayers; but I can explain how they work in light of my own understanding of psychic vampirism. It has to do essentially with what can be called *identification*, which is brought on by envy or jealousy of another's good looks, their beautiful clothes, their new car, even their wit, charm, or sense of humor—anything that a person envies and would like to have for themselves.

Envious people have a strong desire to possess what they strongly *identify* with in other people, and their envy-energy psychically attaches itself to the other person's energy field; which is how they psychically vampirize the vital life force out of the unsuspecting person, who could even be a total stranger just passing by.

This is how one becomes *affascinato,* as we say in Italian; and knowing what I do about man's primordial instinct for survival, I finally solved the mystery of psychic vampirism which I see today as man's highly evolved shadow instinct. So my experience with my mother went a long way to helping me protect myself from man's collective shadow, which I came to call "Old Whore Life" that loves to screw us of our "virtue"—or, vital life force if you will; and having said this, I can begin to unravel the mystery of the secret way of life...

The secret way of life did not reveal itself to me in a moment of glorious enlightenment, but in tiny sparks of revelation every time I mined another nugget of spiritual gold out of the impervious rock of life, and many of life's experiences were less than kind to me; in other words, I *had* to live the secret way of life to find the secret way, and it all started when I stepped off the breakwater that memorable day with my *Royal Dictum* and began the long and anguishing journey of "dying" to the pleasures of my life.

When all is said and done, as I lived my *Royal Dictum* I became increasingly more sensitive to my unconscious self, as well as the unconscious side of life; so sensitive, in fact, that I began to sense the shadow side of everyone's personality. And the more sensitive I became, the more my sensitivity evolved into a kind of sixth sense, or psychic sight if you will; which made my life very interesting, because now I began to see the dynamic play of the shadow side of life between people like watching a play within a play, especially the shadow psycho-drama between my mother and father whose marriage was fraught with so much unresolved energy that it made life very difficult for the family.

But I'm getting ahead of myself in my story. I just wanted to reveal that waking up to the shadow side of life comes with the quest for one's true self; because one cannot find one's true self unless they confront their own shadow, and living my *Royal Dictum* forced me to confront my own shadow and integrate it into my life; and that's how I began to awaken to the secret way of life that taught me how to make the two into one.

This is the mystery of what Carl Jung came to call the individuation process, because one cannot become their true self without integrating their shadow into their conscious personality, which is what Jesus meant by making the two into one; but the shadow does not want to be integrated into the conscious personality, and there's always hell to pay when one tries to tame the shadow energies of one's unconscious self. That's how I came to my saying, *the shortest way to God is through hell!* Now, about the secret way of life?

After all the thought that I have given to this mystery, which is central to every spiritual teaching in the world, and all the books that I have written to give it creative expression, I've come to the conclusion that there's only one way to reveal what it is, and that's to just come right out and say it; and as elusive and mysterious as it may appear to be, **the secret way is the vital force of life that flows from the Godhead through life and back to the Godhead again, and as it flows back to the Godhead defines the nature of the secret way, which is why I have called the secret way inherently self-transcending.**

The secret way is a state of consciousness, which one has to call spiritual; but the paradox of the secret way is that it *is* its own way to itself, and the only way to this state of consciousness—which, putting all of my cards on the table, is the Godhead—is to live the secret way. Let's take one of Christ's sayings: ***"But when thou dost alms, let not thy left hand know what the right hand doeth: That thine alms may be in secret: and thy Father, which seeth in secret himself shall reward thee openly"*** (Matthew 6: 3-4).

Jesus is speaking in code. He is revealing how the secret way works to bring one to his true self and the Godhead. The principle dynamic of the secret way is the power of inherent self-transcendency; meaning, as one lives the secret way one taps into the power that lifts one up to a higher state of consciousness. So, let's break down the code of Christ's saying to see how the secret way of life works in the simple act of giving charity.

By "left hand" Jesus means our unconscious shadow self, the *non-being* part of our personality; and by right hand, Jesus means the conscious *being* part of our personality; but because the self needs energy to grow, our shadow is always on the lookout for energy to grow in its *non-being.* And as unconscious as we may be to our shadow, our shadow is conscious to itself and forever wary of what we do consciously. This is the paradox of our personality; **we are not conscious of our shadow, but our shadow is conscious of us.**

Now, the vital force of life flows through every experience that we have, and doing acts of charity is a magnificent way to tap into the energy of life, because the paradoxical nature of the secret way is that *the more you give of yourself the more of yourself you will have to give,* and conversely *the less you give of yourself the less of yourself you will have to give*; but I will go into this later because it speaks to the paradox of love. For now, suffice to say that doing charity taps into the vital force of life, which our shadow wants for itself; this is why Jesus admonishes us to not vaunt about our works of charity—*because it's in the vaunting of one's charity that gorges the non-being of our shadow personality!*

Our shadow is a mystery, and the only way to get a grip on what makes our shadow tick is that it is driven to *be*. That is the shadow's *raisons d'être,* because the shadow side of our ego personality is the potential *being* of who we strive to be, which is our true self. Our shadow is the *non-being* side of our *being*, and its goal in life is to simply *be;* that's why our shadow seeks all the attention that it can get without giving itself away that it is not who we are. **Our shadow is the self of our non-being, and it is also the non-self of our being.**

In effect, our ego/shadow personality is the naturally evolved dynamic of man's psyche by which we seek to become conscious of our true self, which is our divine nature that comes from the Godhead; and the constant play of our ego and shadow constitutes our *becoming,* because this is how the self grows. But because this natural process of individuation cannot satisfy the longing in our soul to be all that we are meant to be, we have to take evolution into our own hands to complete what nature cannot finish. This is the only way to satisfy the longing in our soul to be all that we are meant to be; which I did as I lived the secret way that I awakened to with my *Royal Dictum*, Gurdjieff's teaching, and the sayings of Jesus.

But this is still such a deep mystery that I must pause for thought…

9. Waking Up to the Shadow

And now we come to the heart of my strange story, the process of waking up to my unconscious self which C.G. Jung called the shadow and which I first became aware of in Gurdjieff's teaching in what he called the "false personality."

By the time I had the initiatory experience that alerted me to my false personality (I hadn't found Jung's teaching yet and wasn't aware of the term shadow), I had read a number of books on Gurdjieff and his teaching that I had ordered from *Samuel Weiser* in New York City, and I was "working" on myself by practicing the techniques of *self-remembering, non-identifying, conscious effort,* and *intentional suffering*—as well as my own edict of self-denial that I called my *Royal Dictum;* but I hit a brick wall that stopped me in my tracks, and I sank into deep despair. And here I must explain with the 20/20 vision of my life today, because this is the only way to make sense of the experience that I had one night that initiated me into the world of the mysterious shadow side of life and my false personality.

So there I was, living at home with my parents and young brother (all of my other siblings had long left home and had their own life in various parts of the country), and I was working hard to get my house-painting business off the ground; but I could make no more headway in my quest for my true self because all the "work" I was doing on myself could take me no further until I became aware of my own shadow. And then I had the experience that shattered my wall and opened me up to the vast horizons of my own potential.

It was so powerful that it shocked me out of myself; but I needed this shock to wake me up to the reality of my situation, because without this shock to my psyche I would have continued to pound my head against the wall and bleed in my despair. I never understood why I had this experience, and I could only describe it as a miracle—which it was; but with 20/20 hindsight, I know now that it was my Higher Self that intervened to help me break through the impenetrable wall of my *non-being* which kept me from finding my true self.

Gurdjieff Was Wrong But His Teaching Works

I didn't know it then, and it took many years to learn how the mysterious dynamic of the guiding force of life works—which I came to see was the divine intelligence of the secret way of life that Jesus metaphorically called the kingdom of heaven and I eventually came to call "the omniscient guiding force of life"—but it spoke to me literally in my own mind that night by asking me a simple, but shocking question: *"Why do you lie?"*

If my memory serves me (which, honestly, I cannot trust), I was sitting in my bedroom in the basement of our family home listening to Beethoven's Ninth Symphony to lift my dejected spirits, and it's quite possible that I heard that voice in my mind at precisely that moment when the symphony climaxed with euphoric triumph in Schiller's Ode to Joy—

"Why do you lie?" I heard loud and clear, in a man's voice that I have never been able to identify. I knew it wasn't Gurdjieff, because it was too clearly English and not accented the way Gurdjieff talked; but whoever spoke got my attention, and I waited for more. But nothing else came, and I waited and waited shocked by what I had just heard. *"What? Me, lie? How absurd,"* I reacted, when the music stopped. *"I'm a truth seeker, I don't lie—"*

But there was so much authority in that voice that it reverberated in my soul with such devastating frequency that it shattered the wall of my *non-being* like the high notes of an opera singer's voice shattering a crystal glass bowl; and this unbelievable experience initiated me into the mysterious *non-being* world of my imperceptible false self...

I have to pause here. I cannot continue my story chronologically, because I have to explain the mysterious process of our *becoming* from the perspective of my life today; that's the only way I can bring clarity to the process of **conscious individuation.**

By **conscious individuation,** I simply mean that one has taken the evolution of their individuating self out of the hands of nature, as it were; because nature can only evolve the self to a certain point, and no further. Nature has to operate within the laws of its own dynamic, two of which are the imperceptible laws of karma and reincarnation; and the energy that we create through karma and reincarnation keeps us fettered to the *enantiodromiac* process of our *becoming*—the *being* and *non-being* dynamic of natural evolution; and the only way to break this cycle of life and death is to learn the secret of self-transcendence that is central to Gurdjieff's teaching and the enigmatic sayings and parables of Jesus.

This is why I heard the voice that night that asked me the question, *"Why do you lie?"* I could not break through the wall of my own *non-being* without becoming aware of my false self, because my false self *was* the wall that kept me from transcending myself; and the only explanation that I have for hearing that voice in my mind asking me why I lied was because of my total and absolute commitment to finding my true self.

I had come to a dead end, and I honestly could not make any more headway with Gurdjieff's teaching and my *Royal Dictum*; so the merciful *I Am Principle of Life*—which is the omniscient voice of the secret way—came to my aid, as it does for every soul that is ready to realize its destiny of singleness of wholeness of self; and asking me the question *"Why do you lie?"* gave me the impetus that I needed to continue my quest for my true self.

Of course, I was completely blind to how life worked when I had this experience; but since then I have learned that many people have had miraculous experiences by way of dreams, meaningful coincidences (which Jung came to call "synchronicities"), visions, and seemingly innocuous life-changing happenstances that eventually forced me to conclude that there is a divine intelligence to life that guides us on our destined journey to our true self. In fact, there are many books today that address this very premise, like Robert H. Hopcke's book *There Are No Accidents, Synchronicity and the Stories of Our Lives*, and *The Power of Coincidence, How Life Shows Us What We Need to Know*, by David Richo.

"Our lives have a narrative structure, like that of novels," writes Robert H. Hopcke, "and at those moments we call synchronistic this structure is brought to our awareness in a way that has a significant impact upon our lives." And although every soul's story is the same, which is to become who we are meant to be, the journey to our true self is always individual because of our personal karma; and resolving the karma that keeps us trapped in the endless cycle of our *becoming* is what **conscious individuation** is all about. This is what led me to see that we have two destinies: one spiritual, and one karmic; and **conscious individuation** is all about bringing our personal karmic destiny into agreement with our pre-scripted spiritual destiny and making the two into one—which is what Jesus meant with his teaching:

"For when the master himself was asked by someone when his kingdom would come, he said, *'When the two will be one, and the outer like the inner, and the male with the female neither male nor female'*" (*The Unknown Sayings of Jesus*, Marvin Meyer).

Jesus spoke in code, but as I "worked" on myself from the perspective of my newfound self-awareness that energized my quest for my true self that unsuspecting night when I was asked the innocent question that alerted me to my false self, I began to "see" through the veil of mystery that cloaked Christ's teaching of "salvation."

One cannot imagine the powerful effect that simple question *"Why do you lie?"* had upon my life, because from that moment on I was on HIGH ALERT to myself, and I am not exaggerating when I say that Gurdjieff's technique of *self-remembering* took on a completely new meaning for me. It was as though my *self-remembering* efforts had been plugged into a highly charged current of self-awareness that kept me alert to my every thought, my every word, and my every deed—*and I could not believe how false I was!*

It was like I had created what the Buddhists call a 'watcher" self, but in Gurdjieff's teaching was a more highly developed "work" self, and from this much more objective perspective of self-awareness, I found myself "catching" my false self in the middle of a thought, in the middle of a sentence, and in the middle of a deed; that's how I began to see into the unconscious world of *non-being* and my shadow self.

But ironically, regardless how false I now found myself to be (in all honesty, I prefer the word *inauthentic* because it seems to convey the unresolved karmic energy of my *non-being* more accurately), and which made me sick to my stomach every time I caught myself lying or pretending to be more knowledgeable than I was or have more experience than I did, I also saw my unconscious falseness as a challenge to overcome; and every day I went out into the world like a Holy Warrior ready to do battle with my false self!

That's when I made an ideal of William Wordsworth's poem "Character of the Happy Warrior" and added to the ethic of my eclectic spiritual path that I was forging out for myself the most powerful lines that I had read in all of literature: "He labors good on good to fix, and owes /To virtue every triumph that he knows: /—Who, if he rise to station of command, /Rises by open means; and there will stand /On honorable terms, or else retire, /And in himself possess his own desire." And I grew in "virtue" with every effort that I made!

I don't know when it happened, but my unrelenting efforts to catch my false self in my daily affairs, especially with the people I painted for—*and, believe me, my shadow became increasingly more clever, devious, and harder to catch with my every effort to transform the consciousness of my falseness by being more honest, truthful, and less pretentious!*—made me so self-aware that I finally apprehended what Gurdjieff meant by truth and lying in one of his talks to his pupils, which Ouspensky secretly recorded for the book he would write one day: "To speak the truth is the most difficult thing in the world; and one must study a great deal and for a long time in order to be able to speak the truth. The wish alone is not enough. *To speak the truth one must know what the truth is and what a lie is, and first of all in oneself.* And this nobody wants to know" (*In Search of the Miraculous,* P. D. Ouspensky, p. 22).

This may be hard to believe, but I was so relentless in my efforts to authenticate my life that I brought myself to the point of self-awareness where I *knew* instantaneously when I was lying to myself and to others; but, believe it or not, I still had an excruciatingly long way to go before I broke the hold that my shadow had upon my psyche. And this brings me to my remarkable experience in the Nipigon Inn Hotel where I was waiting on tables while stripers danced seductively on stage that illustrates the incredible power of Gurdjieff's teaching; but I will relate this experience when I have provided a little more context…

Gurdjieff Was Wrong But His Teaching Works

As I said, I left university because I was called back into the world to find my true self, and I have to conjecture that my Higher Self was aware of what kind of life I would have had had I continued with my studies in philosophy and saw that it would be better for me to go back out into the world and forge a path that would be more propitious to my task, which I did with Gurdjieff's teaching, my *Royal Dictum,* and the sayings of Jesus; so my experience that night in the Nipigon Inn Hotel was not unexpected given my intention.

Given that I accomplished my goal of finding my true self, I can tell the story of my quest for my true self with the certainty of the outcome; and I can say without equivocation that I would never have accomplished my goal had I not had the courage to do what I was called upon to do, however at odds it seemed to be with conventional thought or reason. But I got consolation from people like Alfred A. Orage, who sacrificed his brilliant career as editor and publisher of his highly respected *New Age* journal to go to France to study Gurdjieff's teaching; and Dr. Maurice Nicoll, who left his studies with C. G. Jung and went to Fontainebleau to "work" on himself also under Gurdjieff's unforgiving tutelage, and there were many others who heeded the call to seek Gurdjieff out for what he had to offer. But why? What did Gurdjieff have that pulled so many highly successful and creative people to his teaching; doctors, writers, and artists? What did he have that they were missing?

This question has to be answered before I continue with my story, because it speaks to the natural process of individuation which cannot satisfy the longing in man's soul to be all that he is driven to become. This would all be philosophical speculation had I not experienced what I did in my quest for my true self; but because I *experienced* where souls come from and that we are all encoded to become conscious of our divine nature that the natural process of individuation cannot satisfy, I *know* that when one has evolved as far as nature can take him he has to find a way to satisfy the longing in his soul that will not go away, and Gurdjieff offered a way to satisfy this unbearable longing. That's why people went to him. Like me, they were desperate; and desperate people will do desperate things to get what they need.

In *Modern Man in Search of a Soul,* Carl Jung wrote: "About a third of my cases are suffering from no clinically definable neurosis, but from the senselessness and emptiness of their lives. It seems to me, however, that this can well be described as the general neurosis of our time. Fully two-thirds of my patients have passed middle age." If this was so when Jung published his book in 1933, I venture to say that this feeling of senselessness and emptiness is much more pronounced in people's lives today, which accounts for the proliferation of spiritual teachings and self-help movements that have flooded the marketplace; but still, the soul longs for more. Why? And just what is this "more" that soul longs for?

Logically, if one feels that his life is empty and senseless then it follows that what he longs for is MEANING. In fact, this was the very thing that drove George Ivanovich Gurdjieff to go out into the world and search for twenty years with a group of fellow seekers to answer the question that burned inside him: **"What is the sense and significance of life on Earth and human life in particular?"** And Gurdjieff, who at an early age awakened to a profound experience of the "whole sensation" of himself, a deep, dimensional self-remembering that became the foundation of his *being*, found the answer that he was looking for in hidden esoteric schools that he drew upon to create his Fourth Way teaching; but as much love, respect, and admiration that I have for this remarkable man who changed my life, I *know* from my own quest for my true self that Gurdjieff was wrong to found his teaching upon the premise that man is not born with an immortal soul, but correct in his understand that man can "create" his own soul with *conscious effort* and *intentional suffering*. And herein lies the quandary that perplexes every seeker who longs for wholeness and completeness, and the inspiration for writing this strange story of my quest for my true self.

The process to realize our true self is not difficult to find, because the secret way is the basis of all spiritual teachings; but not until one *lives* the spiritual principles of a teaching will one transform the consciousness of his *being* and *non-being* and "create" their own immortal soul which Jesus called the making of the two into one and Jung called "mystical marriage" that he had learned from breaking the code of ancient alchemist texts and later confirmed in his commentary on Richard Wilhelm's translation of the ancient Taoist text *The Secret of the Golden Flower*. So as fascinating as Gurdjieff was to me, it was his teaching that set me on my journey to my true self, because by

Gurdjieff Was Wrong But His Teaching Works

"working" on myself I transformed the consciousness of my false self and broke the hold that my shadow had upon my psyche; and I'm not speaking metaphorically, because I actually experienced the "snap" inside me that night in the Nipigon Inn Hotel when my shadow was forced to set me free.

Everything came to a head that night. I had worked all day on my day job painting, I had a bad summer cold that I couldn't shake, and as I tended to my customers in my evening job at the Nipigon Inn Hotel I did so under the unbelievable duress of *non-identifying* with my cold, my work, and the seductive women dancing on the stage; but to understand why I experienced what I did that night I have to explain the dynamic principle of Gurdjieff's impossible technique of *non-identifying*, which I came to see was the most effective way to "catch" the energy that I needed to "create" my own soul.

Remember, I had learned by this time that the self needed energy to grow; and the technique of *non-identifying* afforded the most efficient way to what Socrates so aptly referred to as "gathering and collecting" soul into itself, and I *non-identified* with my cold and my customers and especially the strippers whose naked bodies so excited me sexually that I had to make superhuman efforts to *non-identity* with my desire for sexual pleasure. Although I had been living my *Royal Dictum* for quite some time by now, I still had to make superhuman efforts to *non-identify* with my sexual desires; and by this I mean that I had somehow miraculously mastered a way to "withdraw" myself from the objects of my desire and go to a neutral place that I came to call my "sanctuary" where not even God could reach me.

So there I was tending to my customers as the strippers gyrated their naked body on stage to the blare of their musical selections, caught in the grips of a summer cold that begged for me to go home and have a hot cup of Echinacea Tea and curl up in bed; but true to the principle of the Fourth Way, which was to use every situation in life to your advantage, I made superhuman efforts that night to *non-identify* with my work, my cold, and the strippers, and then it happened: I felt a "snap" inside me, and instantly I was set free from myself!

I *actually* felt a "snap" inside me, and I *actually* felt myself liberated from what I knew was also myself—but only in my liberation I KNEW that I was more free than I had ever been in my entire life, like I had stepped out of myself like a snake shedding its old skin, and it wasn't until many years later that I realized that it was my archetypal shadow that had "snapped" from the mounting pressure of all the liberating energy that I had "created" with my superhuman efforts to *non-identify* with my cold, my customers, and the strippers. But this requires an explanation, because it is much too esoteric to understand...

To the outside world, it looked like Gurdjieff was running a madhouse at his Institute for the Harmonious Development of Man in Fontainebleau; and the Parisian intelligentsia sarcastically referred to the people there as the "forest philosophers." This was in the 1920s, the same time that my high school hero and literary mentor Ernest Hemingway was living in Paris and writing articles for the *Toronto Star* and honing his craft in his favorite cafes which inspired some of his best stories, like "A Clean Well-Lighted Place" and gave him the experiences for his melancholy memoir *A Moveable Feast* that he completed shortly before taking his own life with his favorite shotgun in Ketchum, Idaho. Paris had become the home of many ex-patriot writers like F. Scott Fitzgerald, James Joyce, Ezra Pound and others—all of whom I was reading because I was still driven to become a writer one day; so I devoured everything that I could find on Gurdjieff and his teaching, because my calling to find my true self and my calling to become a writer found a happy meeting place in Paris, France.

That's why I was excited to read *Boyhood with Gurdjieff*, by Fritz Peters; because he had been adopted by Jane Heap and his mother's sister Margaret Anderson, founder and publisher of *The Little Review* that published many writers who were to become famous one day—James Joyce, T. S. Eliot, Ernest Hemingway, F. Scott Fitzgerald, Wyndham Lewis, Ford Maddox Ford, A.R. Orage and others; and Margaret Anderson and Jane Heap sought Gurdjieff out and became members of a special group of women called "The Rope" that Gurdjieff had formed to study his teaching under his tutelage while he studied them. So I became very familiar with life at Gurdjieff's Institute in Fontainebleau, because many of his students wrote about what life was like under Gurdjieff's masterly rule; but the

Gurdjieff Was Wrong But His Teaching Works

irony of Gurdjieff's teaching was that no-one seemed to grasp why he taught the way he did, like getting A. R. Orage to dig a ditch for hours on end day in and day out and then fill it up again.

That's what led people to think that he was running a madhouse. But from my perspective so many years distant, and with my self-initiated drive to "create" my own soul, I understood exactly what Gurdjieff was doing by driving his students the way he did—because he wanted them to accomplish EXACTLY what I had done that night in the Nipigon Inn Hotel when I pushed myself so hard that I "created" enough of that special kind of energy that I came to call "virtue" that it forced my archetypal shadow to release me from my bondage to my *non-being*—the unresolved ego-consciousness of my true self. And herein lies the mystery of Gurdjieff's teaching, which he himself wasn't even aware of—if one has the audacity to imagine that. But it's not audacity, really; it's gnostic certainty.

Let me explain. Gurdjieff's teaching is founded upon the premise that man does not have an immortal soul, and that he must "create" it with *conscious effort* and *intentional suffering*—which is why he pushed his pupils so hard, like having A. R. Orage dig a ditch and fill it back up again with no explanation why he was asked to do it. But Orage had so much faith in Gurdjieff that he worked himself to utter exhaustion, and lo and behold if he didn't experience a "snap" inside himself just as I had that night in the Nipigon Inn Hotel!

That's why Orage had so much respect for Gurdjieff that he called him the "sanest" man he had ever met and his teaching "sublime common sense," because Orage had penetrated Gurdjieff's secret; and he went on to teach and promote Gurdjieff's teaching in America until Gurdjieff did one more thing to get Orage to stand on his own two feet and stop depending upon him: he placed Orage in an impossible situation, and Orage left Gurdjieff and went back to England to live his own life free of Gurdjieff's psychic hold upon him. That's why people believed that Gurdjieff was cruel to his pupils; but was he?

Gurdjieff's goal was to provide conditions for people to "create" their own soul, this is why he was so hard on his pupils; because he knew that it took relentless *conscious effort* and unending *intentional suffering* to accomplish that goal, and very few if any of his pupils did; at least, not that I have read. But whether one knew it or not, Gurdjieff's teaching went a long way to making one ready for the secret way; and one day God willing I'll fly to Paris and go to Fontainebleau-Avon and place a yellow rose on Gurdjieff's grave.

10. My Call to Writing

I was called to writing before I was called to become a seeker, but my poem *Noman* that I wrote in high school changed all of that. Because *Noman* called me to a higher purpose, I had no choice but to go where I was called; but I didn't go willingly. Like Cleanthes said in his prayer to Zeus, I refused to go willingly and was dragged by my destiny to find my true self; but I never gave up on writing. Writing was my dream, and much more.

In the Gurdjieffian spirit of the "way of the sly man," I used writing as a cover story for my quest for my true self, because I was forever buying books and reading; but writing proved to be no less efficacious in my quest for my true self than Gurdjieff's teaching of "work on oneself." I didn't know it then, but having written eight novels and several memoires and books of essays I know now that there is something mystical about writing that speaks to the creative process which Rollo May in his book *The Courage to Create* called "holy," and I have to expound upon my call to writing because writing was how I tapped into the creative life stream that connected me with my inner self. In a word, writing became *my* way.

This is the mystery of the writer's calling; but to explain this mystery I have to connect all the dots to show the big picture of soul's evolution through life. I don't quite know where to begin, but as Robert H. Hopcke said in *There Are No Accidents, Synchronicity and the Stories of Our Lives*, "even the road to nowhere leads somewhere." So it doesn't really matter where I start; like all good writers, I'm simply going to abandon to my creative unconscious and let the spirit of my strange story take me to where it wishes to go…

In her book *The Unknowable Gurdjieff*, Margaret Anderson, who published some of the most original writers of the day in *The Little Review*—Joyce, who wrote *Ulysses*, said to be the best novel ever written; T. S. Eliot, author of *The Wasteland*, "one of the most important poems of the 20th century"; and Ernest Hemingway, whose "simple" style influenced a generation of writers—embraced

Gurdjieff's belief that man is not born with an immortal soul; but, ironically, having a keen eye for the creative process thanks to all the brilliant writers that she published in her *avant-garde* magazine, Margaret Anderson intuited the inherent dynamic of the individuation of soul through life in the very process of making art which necessarily engages what Jung called the "transcendent function" that resolves the *being* and *non-being* of one's nature and makes the artist more true.

"A man may be born an artist—that is, with an art tendency—but he won't have an art until he has worked at art, developed it through an organic process of growth. He must live a life of Art. In the same way, a man can't have a soul until he has lived a life of the Soul," wrote Anderson in *The Unknowable Gurdjieff*.

Without realizing it, Margaret Anderson speaks to the paradox of Gurdjieff's teaching in her metaphor of living art and "creating" one's own soul, because one has to take evolution into their own hands to realize their true self, or "create" their own soul as Gurdjieff and Anderson would have it, which the artist does naturally when he engages the "transcendent function" of his art. This is what makes writing "spooky," to borrow a word from Norman Mailer's memoir *The Spooky Art: Thoughts on Writing;* but what is this mysterious process that Jung called "transcendent function," because this is key to understanding the mysterious process of creative writing—and all the arts, for that matter?

But before I explore this, I'd like to share what I've come to believe to be **Jung's most important discovery**; because as I grew to understand the great psychologist I began to see that everything that he discovered about the psyche flowed from his discovery of the inherent narrative of man's individuation through life, or what Jung simply called one's "story," which finally gave up its secret to me of why writers are compelled to write stories.

Jung made this fortuitous discovery while he was working as a young psychiatrist under Dr. Bleuler at the Burgholzli psychiatric hospital in Zurich. Unlike his colleagues, Jung genuinely wanted to know what went on in the mind of his mental patients; and he puzzled his way through all the confusion of their gibberish, fantasies, hallucinations, delusions and dreams until it dawned on him that there was a narrative structure to their private life that had been interrupted by some unfortunate trauma that caused a psychotic break with reality, and the only cure that he could see was to reconnect his patients with their life story.

I chanced upon this precious piece of information about Jung's discovery in Laurens van der Post's memoir *Jung and the Story of Our Time* when Laurens, whose friendship Jung relished because of their common interest in Africa and primitive cultures, shared with Jung his life-long relationship with the Bushmen, the first people of South Africa who passed on the wisdom of their ancient culture through stories which contained the "seed and essence of their history, their present and future," and the moment I read this a great weight was lifted off my shoulders because I suffered from the double burden of not knowing what drove each and every one of us to do what we do and why writers are compelled to write their stories—both mysteries solved in one brilliant stroke by the compassionate young psychiatrist who would one day become one of history's most distinguished healers.

"As far as we can discern, the sole purpose of human existence is to kindle a light in the darkness of mere being. It may even be assumed that just as the unconscious affects us, so the increase in our consciousness affects the unconscious," wrote Jung in *Memories, Dreams, Reflections*; and the luminous light that Carl Gustav Jung kindled in the darkness of mere being with his life-long study of the psyche awakened us to our own story, which is to become who we are meant to be. "An acorn must become an oak tree and not a donkey," said Jung, realizing that the purpose of life is to be our true self, and which by happy coincidence just happens to be the same teleological driving force that compels writers to write their stories because writing connects them with their unconscious self that completes them.

That's why I was driven to write. I didn't know this at the time, but for years I carried a pocket notebook with me everywhere I went and would stop anytime to jot down notes until one of my customers informed me one day that people were afraid to talk with me because of my inveterate note-taking—which, so the story goes, was probably why James Joyce used to sneak off to the washroom in the pubs he frequented to scribble down bits and pieces of conversation for the stories he would one day make famous in

Dubliners; but in truth, I carried a notebook with me everywhere I went because I wanted to record my impressions and feelings about myself as I "worked" on myself with Gurdjieff's techniques of *non-identifying, self-remembering, conscious effort*, and *intentional suffering*. But for the sake of my business, I had to stop taking notes while working in people's homes, because I could not afford to jeopardise my livelihood. Nonetheless, all of my note-taking helped to create a direct connection with my unconscious, which made creative writing so much easier; and this opens up the door to the mystery of the **transcendent function**…

Without the transcendent function, there would be no individuation; and without the individuation process, we would not become who we are meant to be. In the simplest terms possible, **what Jung meant by transcendent function was the union of the conscious with the unconscious,** which happens quite naturally in our work and daily life; but when we engage the **transcendent function** through creative effort like writing, painting, or playing music we connect with our unconscious so effectively that we transcend ourselves, because in the union of our inner and outer self we realize our Higher Self—which can be frightening.

This is why so many artists destroy their lives with alcohol and/or drugs, because they cannot assimilate the energies of their Higher Self into their ego personality; which became the theme of my literary memoir *The Lion that Swallowed Hemingway*—a play upon Jung's quip on the shadow that overwhelms the ego: "How do you find a lion that has swallowed you?" But I'd prefer to make my point about the **transcendent function** with a musing that I wrote for my spiritual musings blog, because it speaks to the terror of our *becoming*:

Time's Winged Chariot

Age happens to everyone. No one is exempt. We all get older by the day, and one day we're shocked to learn that we aren't what we thought we were; and the mind begins to play funny games with us. Little worries become big worries, and we

Gurdjieff Was Wrong But His Teaching Works

fall into despair. That's what happened to me recently, which not surprisingly brought to mind the foreboding lines from Andrew Marvell's poem "To His Coy Mistress"—But at my back I always hear/Time's winged chariot hurrying near; /And yonder all before us lie /Deserts of vast eternity..."

Life forced it upon me, and I stared into the face of my inevitable demise; but thank goodness it wasn't imminent. At least not that I was aware of, because one must make allowances for Providence which can snatch us anytime. Nonetheless, I despaired at the loss of the vitality of my life before my open heart surgery, because that was the deep well of my inspiration; and I had to reconnect with myself to dispel the lassitude of enervating anxiety, but how? That's the subject of today's spiritual musing...

Writing has always been my inspiration; but the irony of the creative process is that you have to engage it for it to engage you, and I hit a snag while working on the chapter "The Secret Way of Life" of the new book that I'm writing, and despite my best efforts I could not break through my creative blockage; that's why I fell into despair.

Whenever this happened prior to my heart condition, I always engaged my creative energies by physical activity (*how many rotten days I salvaged with a long distance run, I cannot remember!*), but now it's not possible, because whenever I exert myself physically I tax my heart and get instantly winded; and my inactivity only fueled my despair. And every morning I tried to engage my inspiration by writing through my creative blockage, but to no avail; and my little worries became big worries, because much gathers more.

But I am resourceful, as I've had to be in my quest for life's meaning that finally yielded itself to me and which I wrote about in *The Summoning of Noman*, and I employed another means to engage my inspiration by practicing what Jung called "active imagination," a bold but effective method of resolving the conflict between my conscious and unconscious self that became the premise of my book *The Man of God Walks Alone*, and my creative unconscious reminded me of my literary accomplishments which broke up the static energies of my creative blockage and I brought "The Secret Way of Life" to closure.

"God, it feels good to be back!" I exclaimed, when I re-connected with my inspiration; and the creative energies began to flow freely again, and all my demon fears began to disappear. And then, as the merciful law of synchronicity would have it, I was nudged to go online to watch Iain McNay's interview with Jenny Boyd on *Conscious TV*, and something that Jenny Boyd said about the guitarist Eric Clapton confirmed my experience of re-connecting with the source of my creative energy when I engaged my transcendent function.

Jenny Boyd had interviewed Eric Clapton for her book (co-authored with Holly George-Warren) *It's Not Only Rock'n' Roll: Iconic Musicians Reveal the Source of Their Creativity*, and something that Eric Clapton said about his gift for music, which frightened him so much that it drove him to drink, brought my realization of the impenetrable secret of our creative energies full circle, right back to the source from where it comes—God.

Jenny Boyd knew Eric Clapton well, because he was married to her sister; and she knew him before and after his heavy drinking days, and she always thought that he was a special man because of his incredible gift for music; but Eric didn't think he was special at all, because he credited his gift to the source of our creative energies which he said terrified him whenever he got swept away in the flow of his inspiration. *"It's like staring into the Face of God,"* he said to Jenny Boyd, which humbled the iconic musician. But why was Eric Clapton frightened by his gift? And not only him, but every gifted person in the world that is driven by their *daemon* to create?

Jenny Boyd quoted the psychologist Rollo May, who wrote *The Courage to Create*, in her effort to understand Eric Clapton and all the gifted musicians that she interviewed. **"If you don't use your creativity, you betray yourself,"** she said, quoting Rollo May; which was the theme that I explored in my memoir *The Lion that Swallowed Hemingway*, because my high school hero and literary mentor was tortured by the moral demands that his gift for writing placed upon him; and, sad to say, in one way or another he sacrificed all of his relationships both personal and professional upon the alter of his creative genius which garnered him the Nobel Prize for Literature in 1954 and created the insufferable conflict with his unconscious shadow and ego personality that drove him to drink to ease the guilt of all his betrayals and self-betrayals, and depression finally drove him to take his own life as so many gifted artists do who cannot come to terms with the genius of their talent.

And I agreed with Jenny Boyd in her understanding of the awesome power of the creative process, which can make or destroy a gifted artist; but in my quest for life's meaning, I came to see that the choices we make shape who we are, and if we make choices that feed the shadow side of our personality we will have hell to pay, like my mentor Ernest Hemingway whose ravenous ego destroyed his life. "He's a pathological liar, and the cruelest man I know" said his third wife Martha Gellhorn, the only wife to leave the great man to pursue her own career in journalism and creative writing.

That's why Jungian analyst Liz Greene said, "The shadow is both the awful thing that needs redemption, and the suffering redeemer who can provide it," and when I brought "The Secret Way of Life" to closure, my Muse—the voice of my inspiration—provided me with the title of my next chapter, "Waking Up to the Shadow" whose theme is going to be how we can redeem ourselves from our own shadow, which ever artist has to do to be true to their talent; but that's another musing for another day, depending upon my Muse. We may never be ready for Time's Winged Chariot, then; but we can try to meet it half way.

Reading "Time's Winged Chariot" again, I realized that I hadn't quite made my point about my call to writing, because the call to connect with one's creative self is the call to one's own path; and not until I brought my memoir *The Summoning of Noman,* which is the true story of my parallel life, to closure did I realize that I was finally free to speak with my own authorial voice and not with the voice of all the teachings that I had lived and studied, and it was one final symbolic dream that brought closure to *The Summoning of Noman* that confirmed the reality of my life's accomplishment—just as one dream at the end of his life confirmed Carl Jung's life's accomplishment of having realized wholeness and singleness of self, and this opens up the door to my next chapter on **the way of the dream**…

11. The Way of the Dream

I'm not a dream expert, and I don't believe anyone can be because the way of the dream is too vast for anyone to encompass with their mind, however brilliant. Carl Jung spent his whole life trying to puzzle out the way of the dream (he said that he analyzed over sixty thousand dreams in his life), and he gave us a body of knowledge that goes a long way to helping us understand our dreams; but, in the end, the most that he could say about dreams was that they are "the speech of my soul," as they are for everyone.

"Dreams pave the way for life, and they determine you without you understanding their language. One would like to learn this language, but who can teach and learn it?" wrote Jung; and with this proviso, I'd like to offer what the "speech of my soul" said to me to bring my memoir *The Summoning of Noman* to closure, and what my soul said to me in two separate but related dreams months later to confirm the imperative of my dream message that my path in life now is to be the creative writer that I've always longed to be.

Not everyone is born to their path, but those who are know that they are called to their destiny and are driven to realize their soul's desire. From the earliest age, the legendary Canadian figure skater/painter Toller Cranston knew what he wanted to be. "I have always had a sense of my own destiny," he proudly boasted, and he went on to change the face of skating with the graceful fluidity and emotional intensity of a ballet dancer that took the world by storm and inspired generations of champion skaters; but his rise to stardom threw his life out of balance, because he could not assimilate his obsessive shadow energy that drove him with *daemonic* fury to skate until it broke his heart when he failed to be acknowledged for the genius of his artistry and which drove him into deep depression but which he finally managed to control by pouring himself totally into his art (it is said that he painted 70,000 paintings, but that's a gross exaggeration; perhaps 7,000), and he died at the age of 65 at his home in San Miguel de Allende, Mexico of an apparent heart attack but far from being resolved with his soul's desire to be acknowledged for the artistic genius he believed himself to be.

The same can be said of my literary mentor Ernest Hemingway who knew from an early age that he wanted to be a writer, and by the age of twenty-five had honed his own unique style of writing which garnered him the 1954 Nobel Prize in Literature, "for his mastery of the art of narrative, most recently demonstrated in *The Old Man and the Sea*, and for the influence that he has exerted on contemporary style" said the Nobel committee, an original style that the brilliant young writer once called "cablese" (he dispatched his journalism articles from Europe to the *Toronto Star* by cable and loved the unadorned simplicity of this pared-down type of writing) which I tried for years to emulate but had to abandon because I felt stifled by Hemingway's style; but because I was also called to become a seeker, I poured my best energies into finding my true self and not into writing.

Well, I did find my true self; and having satisfied my heart's desire to be what I came into this world to become, I began to pour my energies into the writer that I also wanted to be but couldn't because I did not have a voice of my own; that's why my final dream in *The Summoning of Noman* revealed that having found my true self I now had my own authorial voice and could write from my own unique perspective like all born writers.

I could relate my dream here to make the point, but if I do I'd spoil the climactic ending to *The Summoning of Noman;* so suffice to say that the message of the final dream of my memoir was that I had fulfilled my soul's desire to find my true self and that I was now free to be the writer that I always longed to be but couldn't because I didn't have a voice of my own, which is the stamp of all true writers; and to impress this point upon me, my unconscious gave me two more dreams that told me that my destiny now was to write stories, because in my quest for my true self I had learned the mystical secret of story that every true writer knows but cannot explain because they are blind to their own talent and call it "spooky," as the novelist Martin Amis did when interviewed for his novel *The Zone of Interest*. But this is a mystery that I have to explain to continue with my strange story.

Gurdjieff Was Wrong But His Teaching Works

I've always been intrigued by talent, and envious of people born with it; and not until I found my true self did I began to appreciate the mystery of the individuation process that gives birth to individual talent. But only because I believed in karma and reincarnation; otherwise I'd still be puzzling over why people like the brilliant innovator Toller Cranston and the precocious young Hemingway were born with talent while I had to run the race just to get to the starting line, which speaks to the strange story of my parallel life.

Karma and reincarnation make sense of life, but it takes a long time to wake up to Soul's individuation through karmic reconciliation. I had a dream a few years ago of my future life. I was born with an incredible gift for writing, as precocious as a writer could be, and I had an inordinate fascination with words. I knew intuitively that words were the carriers of knowledge and meaning, and I was reading dictionaries by the age of four and writing stories by the age of five; and I woke up from my dream astonished by my gift for writing.

Scholars have determined that Hemingway's writing vocabulary extended to only nine hundred reader-friendly words, but Hemingway knew big words too. William Faulkner, whom Hemingway bitterly resented because Faulkner won the Nobel Prize for Literature in 1949, five years before Hemingway was awarded his Nobel, accused the globe-trotting he-man Hemingway of being afraid to use big words, and in his pugilistic defense Hemingway, who loved to shadow box with all of his literary competitors, especially giants like Tolstoy and Dostoevsky, snapped back with his knock-out punch: *"You don't need big words to express big emotions."*

Hemingway was a physically centered man with a passion for deep-sea fishing, big game hunting, boxing, bullfighting, drinking, eating, and having sex; and he created a style of writing that best expressed the existential life of man, which is why I could never emulate his "simple" style. I was caught up in my quest for my true self, and aside from reading poetry, novels, and short stories I also read all kinds of spiritual literature and had to find my own style to express my own experiences with life, which is why they say that the style is the man.

But this speaks to the voice of the writer, which has to be heard when it has something to say; this is why writers are compelled to write. Doris Lessing, also a recipient of the Nobel Prize for Literature, said that she could be working in her garden or whatever and enjoy what she was doing, but if she didn't write every day she felt that her day had been wasted; and what drove Toller Cranston to skate and paint with inexhaustible energy if not the same slavish dependence upon the transcendent function that nourishes the artist's soul? And of all his many and excessive passions, Hemingway loved writing most; so what is it about the creative process that drives the gifted person to push themselves beyond their limits?

"The limits of the possible can only be defined by going beyond them into the impossible," said Arthur C. Clarke, the science fiction writer best known for co-writing the screenplay for the movie *2001: A Space Odyssey*; which I had to do to find my true self, and which my unconscious foretold by manifesting the mandala of the "squared circle" of blue and yellow light in my bedroom in my second year of philosophy studies at university.

I pushed myself beyond my limits and did the impossible by "dying" to my life to "find" my life, as Jesus promised with his teaching; and I could not become the writer that I longed to be until I accomplished what I came into this life to do. I never accomplished my goal the first time I lived my life as Orest Stocco, and I chose to return to my same life to try again because this life held too much promise to squander away as I did the first time; and as off the wall as this may seem, I explored this concept of my parallel life in *The Summoning of Noman,* because I knew that by engaging my creative unconscious it would confirm the strange story of my parallel life, which it did. And this speaks to Jung's concept of the transcendent function that is the source of a writer's inspiration and the divine principle of the individuation process that makes us who we are meant to be.

But I can't explain the process of individuation outside the context of karma and reincarnation, because this has been my experience; and I'm telling my story from my own perspective, because this is what I've come to believe about our *becoming*.

Jung contained his understanding of individuation within the paradigm of acceptable science; but even so, he did point to the spiritual dimension of life as he did in his BBC interview when John Freeman asked if he believed in God. "Difficult to answer," he replied. "I know. I do not need to believe; I know." And just a few months before he died, Jung wrote to an English correspondent: "I have failed in my foremost task to open people's eyes to the fact that man has a soul, that there is a treasure buried in the field," which was probably another reason why he came to me in my dream to talk about my book *The Way of Soul.*

From my perspective, then; man is born with an immortal soul. But soul is not fully realized in its own identity until it evolves through life into a fully self-realized spiritual being, just as an acorn seed is not an oak tree until it grows through all the stages and becomes a full grown oak tree; and for soul to realize its full potential we have to grow in the consciousness of our divine nature, which we do naturally through karma and reincarnation.

But karma and reincarnation can only evolve us so far, and no further; and then we have to take evolution into our own hands to complete what nature cannot finish. This was Jung's conundrum, because we cannot transcend the *being* and *non-being* of our *becoming* through karmic reconciliation alone. This can only be accomplished by living the secret way of life, which I found in Gurdjieff's teaching of *conscious effort* and *intentional suffering* and Christ's teaching of "dying" to my life to "find" my life, which quite by "chance" I did unwittingly with my *Royal Dictum*. That's how I found my true self.

So, just what is the mystery of the transcendent function that has the divine power to unite the unconscious with the conscious in a mystical way and "make the two into one," as Jesus would say? What exactly is this dynamic of the transcendent function?

After all the philosophical inquiry and metaphysical study and Gurdjieffian practice of *self-remembering, non-identifying, conscious effort,* and *intentional suffering,* I distilled my understanding of conscious individuation into one simple principle: **the more you give of yourself, the more of yourself you will have to give; and the less you give of yourself, the less of yourself you will have to give.** This is the paradoxical dynamic of our *becoming.*

In effect, we are both *being* and *non-being.* This is our ontology, the essential nature of the consciousness matrix that makes up the "I" of our individuality. Our individual "I" is both our inner and outer self. Our inner self is the evolving identity of our Soul self, and our outer self is our ego/shadow personality that is both conscious and unconscious and different with each new life that we live. This is what creates the karmic dynamic of our *becoming;* and the purpose of our *becoming* is to realize wholeness and singleness of self—or, as Keats would say, "a bliss peculiar to each one by individual existence." But our inner and outer self are not separate selves, as the world would have us believe; they are two aspects of the same self, and realizing wholeness and singleness of self is the goal of individuation.

And now it gets tricky, because it is next to impossible to convey the concept of a non-self, which is the self of our *non-being.* Had I not awakened to my non-self, which is the shadow side of our ego personality, I would never have been able to fathom the reality of my *non-being*—or, to express it in the paradoxical language of our *becoming*, the non-reality of my *being*. In effect, by living the secret way I awakened to the process of our *becoming* as I witnessed the dynamic play of my false and real self in my daily life.

This was my private hell, because once I heard that voice in my mind ask me, *"Why do you lie?"* I became hyper sensitive to myself; and what I learned about myself was that my shadow was so much like me that I could hardly tell the difference. But I persisted, until one day I caught the devil by the tail and my shadow lost its power over me because I saw that my shadow was also me, but not the real me; and that's when I began to see the lie from the truth in myself, and very often in other people. And I grew in my awareness of the consciousness of our *being* and *non-being* and the dynamic of our *becoming* in daily life—or the "what is" of the human condition, as the poet Adrienne Rich would say.

It took many years to make sense of our *becoming*, what Jung called the individuation process; and I had to draw upon the insights of many teachings, poetry and literature to put it all together into a perspective that transformed the reality of my experience of finding my true self into a deeper perception of "what is." But when it all fell into place I could not believe the utter simplicity of God's Divine Plan, which is to expand the Consciousness of God through the evolution of Soul through life.

Gurdjieff Was Wrong But His Teaching Works

What made the puzzle of the Soul's evolution through life so perplexing was the dual nature of human consciousness, the *being* and *non-being* aspects of our individual "I". Soul, our divine nature, is our immortal self that began its evolution through life as an atom of God without self-consciousness; and as it evolved through the stages of life from lower to higher life forms, it finally constellated enough consciousness of life (the *I Am* consciousness of Soul, which is the life force) to become aware of itself for the first time in its evolution, as I experienced in my past-life regression to my lifetime as a higher primate; and from lifetime to lifetime, the newly born "I" of God grows and evolves in the *being* and *non-being* consciousness of its human identity (its ego/shadow personality) through the natural process of creating and resolving karma that nourishes its spiritual identity; that's how our Soul self grows through life. But, sadly, the natural process of individuating the dual consciousness of our *being* and *non-being* cannot satisfy our inherent longing to be all that we are meant to be, which is a spiritually self-realized "I" of God, and we have to take evolution into our own hands to complete what nature cannot finish. And this is where teachers of the Way come into one's life, as Gurdjieff came into mine, to initiate one into the secret way that will reconcile the consciousness of one's *being* and *non-being* and make the two into one.

But how? That's the puzzle. Socrates gave us the answer with his insight into the process of self-reconciliation through the act of "gathering and collecting soul into herself" by living a life of virtue, because virtue taps one into what Jesus called the "water of eternal life," which is the inherently self-transcending energy of God that flows through life. This sounds so esoteric and abstruse that one could easily dismiss it as nonsensical; but the proof of this pudding is in the eating, and not until one tastes the "water of eternal life" will one believe the inherently self-transcending power of the secret way.

And herein lies the mystery of the artist's way, because through their passion for art—be it painting, writing, music, dance, skating or whatever—the artist engages the transcendent function of their art and taps into the life force that flows through life like a River of God, which is why Jesus called it the "water of eternal life," and so satisfying is the "water of eternal life" that the artist cannot get enough, and they drive themselves with relentless passion to get all they can to satisfy the longing in their soul to be whole and complete—as the contemporary artist Jerry Wennstrom did until his art could give him no more and he had to find another way to reconcile his *being* and *non-being* to satisfy the desperate longing in his soul, and which he chronicled in his memoir *The Inspired Heart*.

The natural way of art could do no more for Jerry Wennstrom, because the natural way of life cannot reconcile the *being* and *non-being* consciousness of our ego/shadow personality enough to satisfy the longing in our soul to be all that we are destined to be, because the natural way of individuation through life (be it art or whatever) cannot "gather and collect soul" from the *being* and *non-being* consciousness of our ego/shadow personality efficiently enough for our Soul self to become aware of its divine nature, which I experienced in my mother's kitchen one day while she was kneading bread dough on the kitchen table. So, what did I do that Jerry Wennstrom and virtually every artist could not do with their art?

I learned the secret of how to tap into the River of God and drink in the "water of eternal life" by way of Gurdjieff's teaching of "work on oneself," which forced me to take desperate measures and create my *Royal Dictum* that awakened me to the secret way of Christ's sayings; that's how I drank in enough "water of eternal life" to satisfy the longing in my soul to be my true self, which I experienced that day in my mother's kitchen.

And that's exactly what Jerry Wennstrom did when he was driven to take desperate measures and burn all of his art work and give away all of his possessions and abandon to God to satisfy the longing in his soul to be all that he *had* to be; a remarkable story of self-discovery that he recorded in his memoir *The Inspired Heart*, a fifteen year journey of self-initiation into the secret way of life that nourished his hungry soul.

"I was not completely certain that I hadn't abandoned my tribe altogether when I leapt into unknown formlessness," writes Jerry Wennstrom. "I knew my tribe of fellow artists was threatened by my decision to destroy my art. Perhaps I was to discover a new tribe, a creative or spiritual order that I could give myself to. But I did not know how to choose such an order. If I were to find a new art form or seek out a religious tradition, how would I do that and what would it look like? I trusted that such things were up to God, yet secretly I hoped that something might divinely choose me" (*The Inspired Heart*, p. 119).

I knew Jerry Wennstrom's story well, because I had walked the same path of self-discovery by taking extreme measures that made me ready for the secret way of life ("a creative or spiritual order that I could give myself to," intuits Jerry), and I pieced together the mystifying puzzle of how the natural way of life makes one ready for **CONSCIOUS INDIVIDUATION** that the secret way of life initiates one into, as it did Jerry Wennstrom when he abandoned to God to guide his way through life; and I *know* that the only way to satisfy the longing in our soul to be all that we long to be is to transcend the consciousness of our *being* and *non-being* by making the two into one, which Gurdjieff helped me do.

That's why I have so much love and admiration for Gurdjieff, despite the fact that he was wrong in his premise that we are not born with an immortal soul; his teaching worked for me, because it carried me over from the river of life into the inherently self-transcending river of "eternal life" that carried me deeper into myself until I experienced my own immortal soul in my mother's kitchen that fine summer day.

In *Views from the Real World,* Gurdjieff talks of the two rivers of life which flow together but separately, as it were; and he tells us how one can cross over from the river of life into the other river which flows back to God. "You cannot cross over merely because you wish," said Gurdjieff, as he reveals the mystery of the secret way. "Strong desire and long preparation are necessary. You will have to live through being identified with all the attractions of the first river. You must die to this river. All religions speak about this death: 'Unless you die, you cannot be born again'" (*Views from the Real World,* p. 246); which is precisely what Jerry Wennstrom was compelled to do when his art could no longer satisfy the desperate longing in his soul to be all that he *had* to be.

"As a spiritual path, art carried my life as far as it could within the limited scope of determined human effort," writes Jerry Wennstrom. "I knew I could not have given one more ounce of myself to art as worship and have survived. In retrospect, I honestly believe that my survival was at stake—certainly survival of the spirit, perhaps of the body as well" (*The Inspired Heart,* Jerry Wennstrom, p. 119). Jerry had no choice; he had to find a higher path.

Soul *has* to realize itself. This is the teleological dynamic of life. And when life can no longer satisfy the longing in one's soul for wholeness and completeness, one has to go out of their way to satisfy this desperate longing; this is inevitable, and no one can avoid their destiny. But, as Jung realized as he cared for his patients in the Burgholzli Hospital, some people get stuck; and out of compassion for his patients, Jung sought a way to get them unstuck. And he read and studied everything he could get his hands on to help his patients reconnect with their destiny, which he called their life story; and he discovered the ancient alchemists and their secret teaching. And his theory of the individuation process was born, which he brought as far as he could take it. "The great difficulty here," says Jung, "is that no one knows how the paradoxical wholeness of man can be realized. This is the crux of individuation" (*Jung: His Life and Work, A Biographical Memoir*, Barbara Hannah p.315). But Jesus knew, and so did Gurdjieff and anyone who was initiated into the secret way; and this is the heart of my strange story, how I resolved the paradox of the individuation process and found my own authorial voice that the final dream in my memoir *The Summoning of Noman* confirmed, and which my unconscious ensured with two more dreams that convinced me that my path was now creative writing. As "America's greatest psychic" said: **"Dreams work to accomplish two things. They work to solve the problems of the dreamer's waking life. And they work to quicken in the dreamer new potentials which are his to claim"** (*Edgar Cayce on Dreams,* by Harmon H. Bro, Ph.D., edited by Hugh Lynn Cayce); and my dream opened the door for me to claim my potential as a creative writer.

A month or so after I had the dream that confirmed my authorial voice, I had another dream to expand upon my dream message, which I recorded in my book *In the Shade of the Maple Tree*, a literary exercise in what Jung called "active imagination" in which I dialogue with an archetype (or the actual spirit, I cannot say) of St. Padre Pio whom I met through a psychic medium for my spiritual healing that became the basis of my novel *Healing with Padre Pio*; here's the dream that I shared with St. Padre Pio on

Gurdjieff Was Wrong But His Teaching Works

Monday, *July 14, 2014* in my "active imagination" book *In the Shade of the Maple Tree*:

"Good morning, Padre. I'd like to share a dream I had the other night. It was what I can call a "Jungian dream." I say this because it spoke to me in Jungian language, the archetypal language of the unconscious. I was with some people in my dream, two men, one wearing an Australian type hat, a cowboy hat that has become distinctly Australian in its style, and the other man didn't have a hat but was dressed more like a city person, and he gave me the impression that he was an agent of sort, perhaps a literary agent, or a business representative, and there was someone else but he was invisible to me, but he had a jaguar on a leash; and the jaguar came up to me, extending its paw onto my arm, but it did not claw me even though it gave me a fright, and it stared into my face and opened its mouth and I heard a woman's voice coming from deep within the jaguar, and it spoke to me: "Go into the forest and pick pine mushrooms." And then the scene changed. I saw a woman, very smart looking, in her late forties or early fifties, dressed in what looked like safari clothes, and she had a large manila envelope, the kind that I used to mail out a manuscript, and the envelope was slit and it was raining and rain got into the envelope and I was worried that the words on the paper inside would get smudged, but she lifted the envelope and let the water pour out, and then she went away, presumably to mail or deliver it; and that was my dream. Now I'll give you my interpretation and then you can give me yours. The jaguar was my anima, the female side of my soul; and being on a leash told me that my anima has been tamed. I know the jaguar was my anima, because of the woman's voice that spoke when the jaguar opened its mouth and the female voice spoke to me. She told me to go into the forest and pick pine mushrooms. I didn't know there was a mushroom by this name (I looked it up on Google later and found out that pine mushrooms do exist, and they are called by the Japanese name 'matsutake,' which are rare and very expensive mushrooms, even as much if not more than truffles), but I took 'pine mushrooms' to be a symbol for my creative writing, namely my short stories that I have started to write in my new book *Enantiodromia,* and I took 'forest' to be a symbol of my unconscious. So I took the dream to be my unconscious confirming what you told me long ago, that I should be writing the stories that I have been putting off all these years. My unconscious was giving me permission to write them, so I no longer have to doubt myself. What do you think?"

"I would agree. Your unconscious has confirmed where your writing should go, and which your novel The Golden Seed *will prepare the way for you to take because it will give you all the confidence you need to write creatively. That was a wonderful dream, and I concur with your interpretation."*

"And the envelope?"

*"That's your soul telling you to seek out a publisher for your pine mushroom stories. Now that you have completed your literary memoir (*The Lion that Swallowed Hemingway*) and have merged your two paths—your literary calling and your calling to find your true self—into one path of creative writing, you have no choice but to heed the directive from your unconscious. Soul wants you to write stories. That is your path for the rest of your life."*

That was my dialogue with my archetypal spirit St. Padre Pio, which became Chapter 6, "My Jungian Dream," for my book *In the Shade of the Maple Tree*; and on *June 18, 2015* I shared another dream with St. Padre Pio that re-enforced the message from my unconscious that my path in life is to be a creative writer and write stories. This is Chapter 8, "I Dream of Mushrooms Again," for my work-in-progress *The Sign of Things to Come*:

"Good morning, Padre. I'd like to run a dream by you. I believe it is related to another mushroom dream that I shared with you in the first volume of our talks, the one which inspired me to write stories, which I began to do in my book of short stories that I called *Enantiodromia and Other Pine Mushrooms,* and last night's dream seems to compliment my first dream of mushrooms; meaning, it suggests that I'm going to be working on more stories. Anyway, here's what I dreamt last night: I was in our front yard at our home here in Georgian Bay; and in our yard, on the side by our neighbor's driveway, I noticed that mushrooms had sprouted, a lot of nice brown mushrooms that looked like pine mushrooms, the kind I researched when I went online to find out what pine mushrooms looked like because in my first dream of mushrooms I was told by a woman's voice to go into the forest and pick pine mushrooms. Anyway, in my dream last night I started picking the mushrooms and I place them onto a table that was outdoors; and I remember saying to my neighbors if they wanted to have some since I was going to fry some up. I couldn't get over how many there were, some of which were big and healthy looking, and I saw one whose top was so big it split in two. I picked up one half of the top and slit it in two to see if it was wormy, but it wasn't. It was creamy white and healthy. I smelled it, and I thought it would smell of pine, but it didn't; it had a nice, clean fragrance. And then I remember taking out two large books about two feet tall and a foot wide from a shelf near the table, and what that shelf with books was doing there I don't know, it just seemed to be there like the mushrooms, manifesting out of nowhere, and I took out the two big volumes which I knew were reference books, and I opened one to check out the kind of mushrooms I was picking. They were all the same, with a brown top and pale white stem, and I remember checking out what was listed under the letter U. I don't remember anything else of the dream, except the feeling that the mushrooms were good to eat and the awe that I felt for finding so many mushrooms in my yard. Now I'll give you my sense of the dream and you can tell me what you think. I think I got confirmation from my unconscious that I'm going to be ingesting more story material. The mushrooms symbolize new experiences that I will be writing about. The dream suggests more creative writing. More stories. More books. What do you think?"

"That's a fair interpretation. The mushrooms were pine, but not in a pine forest; which indicates that your experiences will be broader, wider and more diverse, from other forests if you will; and the fact that you invited your neighbors and friends to share in a feed of your unexpected harvest suggests that you were surprised by the bounty in your own yard, and that the stories you write will be ingested or read by others. And as to the two big books that you referenced, they suggest a whole library of research on the variety of mushrooms, or stories, which means other experiences beside the kinds of experiences that you wrote about in your first book of mushroom stories; they will be experiences in other forests of your life, some not yet experienced. Your dream suggests a life full of more

creative writing, ensuring that your path of creative writing will be bountiful, enjoyable, and satisfying."

As can be seen by these two dreams that I shared with St. Padre Pio, I've taken my writing to another level by exercising what Jung called "active imagination," a literary exercise not unlike what Neale Donald Walsch did with his *Conversations with God* books; and whether Walsch talked with God and I talked with St. Padre Pio doesn't really matter, because with this method of creative writing one engages his transcendent function and resolves his unconscious with his conscious self, and who could ask for more?

12. Practical Proof that Gurdjieff Was Wrong

It just occurred to me out of the blue one day while re-reading *Many Lives, Many Masters* by Dr. Brian L. Weiss, the man who made past-life regression therapy a reputable healing modality and helped to take the "woo-woo" out of reincarnation that our Judeo-Christian western world has trouble embracing, that this was the practical proof that I was looking for to prove Gurdjieff wrong in his premise that man is not born with an immortal soul, because how many times has a past-life regressionist ever come up blank?

The simplicity of the proof made me laugh, and I had to sit back and ponder the absurdity of Gurdjieff's premise that man is not born with an immortal soul when so many people have written about past-life regressions and NDEs (near-death experiences) and OBEs (out-of-body experiences) and dreams of being visited by deceased loved ones that it's almost anachronistic now to not believe that our physical body is all we are and that when we die we cease to be and become *"merde"* that fertilizes nature, as Gurdjieff believed. Why are people so recalcitrant? Why is it so hard to believe that we are more than our physical body?

Dr. Brian Weiss was a non-believer in reincarnation. "Years of disciplined study had trained my mind as a scientist and physician, molding me along the narrow paths of conservatism in my profession. I distrusted anything that could not be proved by traditional scientific methods. I was aware of some of the studies in parapsychology that were being conducted at major universities across the country, but they did not hold my attention. It all seemed too far-fetched for me," he writes in *Many Lives, Many Masters*, confessing his spiritual obtuseness; and then he met Catherine, the client who changed his life.

Before I mention how Catherine changed his life, I have to make a point about Dr. Weiss's life that speaks to the natural way of life that evolves an individual soul as far as it possibly can to make them ready for the secret way so they can complete their destiny to wholeness and completeness. In all honesty, I didn't know how I was going to make this point which cried out to be made with each chapter that I wrote; but as I always do, I placed my trust in my creative unconscious, and lo and behold if I wasn't given the perfect opportunity to make my point about the natural way of life with Dr. Brian Weiss's serendipitous introduction to reincarnation through his client Catherine. So, what is my point?

My point is that God is merciful. My point is that God does not create the universe by throwing up a switch and letting the universe run by its own laws and leaving us to our own devices, as science would have us believe—*sans God, of course*. My point is that the natural process of individuation through karma and reincarnation does not evolve us as far as it can and then abandons us to find our own way, as my story would suggest; and Gurdjieff's story; and Jung's story; and Jerry Wennstrom's story; and every seeker who comes to the end of the line and feels lost. My point is that the natural way of life evolves soul to the point where the sheer momentum of their own individuation process initiates them into the secret way of life through the goodness of their own nature which every soul called to serve life has proven over, and over, and over again.

"All destiny leads down the same path—growth, love and service," said Dr. Elisabeth Kubler-Ross in *The Wheel of Life, A Memoir of Living and Dying*, which speaks to the natural way of life with the eloquence of a seasoned soul that was taken as far as life could take her through the natural process of individuation through karma and reincarnation—because Dr. Elisabeth Kubler-Ross served life with monumental courage as she broke the stubborn ground of man's spiritual obtuseness with her courageous and career-threatening study of death and dying and near-death experiences.

It's taken a long time to piece out this puzzle, and I would not have solved it had I not gone for a spiritual healing with the psychic medium who channeled St. Padre Pio that I wrote about in my novel *Healing with Padre Pio*; because in one of my sessions with St. Padre Pio, who was one of my psychic medium's spiritual guides (her other guide was an Irish spirit), I asked him a question that ached to be asked. Without looking it up in my novel, which I will do later, in effect my question was: *did you become all knowing and seeing when you crossed over, or did you grow into it gradually in your life before you died?*

Gurdjieff Was Wrong But His Teaching Works

I asked him this because I made a deep study of his life as I prepared for each one of my ten spiritual healing sessions with him, reading all the books that I could get on his life (ten or twelve biographies), plus his own book *Secrets of a Soul, Padre Pio's Letters to His Spiritual Director*, and I was very familiar with the recorded miracles attributed to him while he was still alive, the perfume that Padre Pio emitted for certain people which came to be called "the aroma of paradise," and his out-of-body appearances to people who were sick or dying, plus his own remark that revealed his utter humility. "I am a mystery to myself," he replied, when asked about his spiritual gifts; and I wanted to know if his life of devoted service in Jesus Christ to his fellow man had raised his spiritual consciousness to that of all knowing and seeing instantly when he crossed over, or whether it was a gradual transcendence through what Socrates called the most noble virtue—goodness; and St. Padre Pio's answer confirmed Christ's imperative: ***"Do not store up for yourselves treasures on earth, where moth and rust destroy, and where thieves break in and steal. But store up for yourselves treasures in heaven, where neither moth nor rust destroys, and where thieves do not break in or steal. For where your treasure is there will your heart be also"*** (Matthew 6: 19-21).

Padre Pio initiated himself into the secret way through suffering. His path was *la via di sofferenza*, which is Italian for the way of suffering; and along with all of his bodily ailments that he suffered throughout his life, he suffered the pain of the five holy wounds of Jesus for fifty years. He did not just have the visible signs of Christ's wounds, he actually suffered the pain as well; and he could not get enough of it. "I want to inebriate myself with pain," he confessed, which would make most psychiatrists shudder. But Padre Pio had discovered the secret of the way, and he called his pain "my glory."

I understood what he meant immediately, because by "glory" he meant that he was storing his "treasure" in heaven; and by "treasure" Jesus meant that special energy that I came to call "virtue" that one needs to transcend himself. This is the secret of the Way, and not until one is initiated into the secret way of life will they appreciate why the simple monastic priest from Pietrelcina, Italy would want to inebriate himself with pain.

"My suffering is more precious to me than gold," he revealed to Father Benedetto Nardella, his spiritual director; and he added, "If humanity could realize the value of suffering, they would ask for nothing else" (*Pray, Hope, and Don't Worry, True Stories of Padre Pio*, by Diane Allen, p. 5). But this begs an explanation…

Jesus told Jung's spiritual guide Philemon in Jung's *Red Book* that he had brought "the beauty of suffering" to the world, and I had intended to reserve my understanding of the mystical nature of suffering for the book I hope to write one day called *The Beauty of Suffering, Reflections on Jung's Red Book*; but my creative unconscious is calling for an explanation now to give context to the story of my own transcendence. St. Padre Pio did tell me that I had transcended myself and my spiritual community, and I know that I transcended myself because I had stored enough "treasures" in heaven to lift myself above the consciousness of my ego/shadow personality, just as Padre Pio did; so I have to explain what this means to do justice to the strange story of my *becoming*.

In the simplest terms possible, suffering creates that special kind of energy that we need to grow in our own individual identity; our Soul self, if you will. Jesus called this special kind of energy our "treasures" in heaven, and Padre Pio called it "my glory." I call it "virtue." But it doesn't matter what we call it, this special kind of energy is born of the suffering that we experience when our *being* and *non-being* are brought into conflict by the circumstances of our life—like the time I suffered from the simple lie that I told an Ontario Provincial Police officer when he called me at home to ask me if I had passed a school bus that had stopped on the Trans-Canada Highway to let the children out; one seemingly innocuous little lie that was so unbearably soul-crushing that it ruined my whole summer.

I'd like to write a short story someday on how I anguished over that simple lie, but the gist of it was that I was driving home to Nipigon from a job that I was working on in the adjacent town of Red Rock and I was following a school bus; but I had started to pass the bus before it flagged its sign for the traffic to stop so the driver could let the children out, so I did pass the bus when the stop sign was down but it was too late for me to stop. It was a judgment call, but someone reported my license plate number to the OPP and I got a call that night.

It could have been the bus driver that reported me, but I suspected it was the driver of the car following me because I knew that he had an antipathy for me; not for anything that I had said or done to him, but because my energy affected him in the same way that Jung explained when he said: "If life had led you to take up an artificial attitude, then you wouldn't be able to stand me, because I am a natural being. By my very presence I crystallize; I am a ferment. The unconscious of people who live in an artificial manner sense me as a danger. Everything about me irritates them, my way of speaking, my way of laughing" (*Carl Jung, Wounded Healer of the Soul*, by Claire Dunne, p.22).

The person who was behind me on the highway that day was a deeply closeted gay, and his whole public life was a lie. He knew that I knew, and I could sense his antipathy for me every time we met at his mother's cottage or one of our spiritual functions because he was also a member of our spiritual community that his mother had introduced me to after I moved on from Gurdjieff's teaching; and as much as I respected his life choice, I *knew* that my authenticity was too much for him, and his unconscious sensed a danger in me; that's why I suspect he reported me to the OPP. But to be fair, it could very well have been the bus driver—which, as irony always seems to have it, it probably was. Nonetheless, I suffered anguish all summer long for the lie that I told the OPP officer; but why?

The answer is very simple, and at the same time so complex that it took my whole book *The Summoning of Noman* to make sense of my false self; but because I thought I had become master of my own house after years of indefatigable effort authenticating my life with Gurdjieff's teaching of "work on oneself," my *Royal Dictum*, and the sayings of Jesus I never imagined I could be blind-sided by my shadow ever again, but "Old Whore Life" caught me off guard when the OPP officer called me that night and I panicked and lied.

Of course, the officer could not prove that I was driving my vehicle, so he couldn't pursue the matter any further and let me off with a friendly reminder; but I could not forgive myself for lying, and that goddamn simple lie wormed its way into my soul and constricted my life like a boa constrictor. That's why I was inspired to write *Old*

Whore Life, Exploring the Shadow Side of Karma when Penny and I moved to Georgian Bay years later.

My conscience bothered me. Because my goal in life was to be true to myself, as authentically me as I could be, that simple lie shattered a hole in the fortress of my life and I cursed the wretched "Old Whore" all summer long for screwing me of my virtue. I could not get over my anger at myself for letting my false self get the best of me; and I suffered. That's how much power our shadow has over us, despite how authentic we think we are; and that was a lesson I would never forget because it pared me down and made me wiser. That's just one small example of what Jesus meant by the beauty of suffering; but who can see it?

Padre Pio did. That's why he said, "Believe me, I find happiness in my suffering," because he *knew* the redemptive power of suffering. That's why I had to ask the question I did in my last spiritual healing session with him: "When you crossed over to the Other Side, did you experience spiritual ascendancy the moment you crossed over, or was this a partial process which began in this lifetime?"

And Angie, who channeled St. Padre Pio, replied" "No, it was immediate. He had a bliss, an immediate bliss. As he was passing, he felt nothing but joy, an unadulterated, passionate joy. I can see him glowing, and I'm getting major goose bumps. He's showing me that picture. It was wonderful—" (*Healing with Padre Pio,* pp. 333-4). That's why Padre Pio called suffering "my glory," because suffering brought him closer to God.

Padre Pio is an extreme example of the point I want to make, that **when the way of life can take us no further we are then called to serve life; and in our service to life we grow in the consciousness of our own becoming and transcend ourselves naturally**, just as the humble Capuchin monk who continues to serve life from the Other Side. "After my death I will do more. My real mission will begin after my death," he said, and true to his word, after his death untold miracles have been attributed to St. Padre Pio, and every year millions of pilgrims make their way to San Giovanni Rotondo where Padre Pio lived and died.

There is something magical in one's service to life, something that cannot be put to words because it's next to impossible to conceptualize the inherently self-transcending power of one's goodness in their service to life; but the goodness of one's service can be felt by everyone it touches, like the actor Gregory Peck who touched my life and countless others as a movie actor in such roles as Atticus Finch in Harper Lee's *To Kill a Mockingbird.*

Gregory Peck's life is a perfect example of how the natural process of individuation through karma and reincarnation made him ready for the secret way of life through service as an actor, though he himself was mystified by how he was called to his destiny. But that's how life works: **when one is ready to be called to their destiny, life's comes calling.**

Gregory Peck was a pre-medical student at Berkeley University, California. One day a man came up to him and said: "I'm the director of the Little Theater, and I need a tall actor; and I've seen you on the campus and I wondered if you'd come and have a try."

This director, whom Gregory Peck did not know, was life's messenger calling him to his destiny of service to life through acting; and, unconscious of his own destiny, Peck explained his serendipitous call to destiny in words that make one smile: "I don't know why I did; I just said, well, why not?" And the rest is history.

God is merciful, and life never leaves us stranded because life is not a tale told by an idiot full of sound and fury signifying nothing; it has a logic that we cannot see until we are called to our own destiny, because as we live our destiny we quicken the new potential which is ours to claim as Gregory Peck realized late in his life. "If I'd said no (to the Little Theater director on campus), "or I don't see the point of it, my life would be entirely different," he said in an interview late in his life; but his life of acting fulfilled him as a person and touched so many lives that it's impossible to compute the goodness of his service to the world. As one person said, "Somewhere in that man is the best of all of us," which for me Gregory Peck exemplified as Tom Rath in my favorite movie, *The Man in the Grey Flannel Suit.*

Having shown how the natural way of life prepares us for our destiny, let me return to Dr. Weiss and the practical proof that Gurdjieff was wrong in his premise that man is not born with an immortal soul, because like Gregory Peck Dr. Brian L. Weiss was also called by serendipity to his destiny of serving life through past-life regression therapy, and he grew in love and service and wrote *Messages from the Masters, Tapping Into the Power of Love*.

In Chapter One, he writes: "For those of you meeting me for the first time, a few words of introduction are necessary. I have come a long way from that fateful day when I, a classically trained physician, professor of psychiatry, and confirmed skeptic, realized that human life is grander and more profound than even my rigorous medical training had led me to believe," and he goes on to say something that lends all the practical proof that one could ask for that Gurdjieff was wrong in his belief that we are not born with an immortal soul, because **if reincarnation is a fact of life than everyone must have an immortal soul that is born over and over again to fulfill its destiny of realizing its divine nature.**

Dr. Weiss continues: "Because my work deals with the themes of reincarnation, past-life regression therapy, and the reunion of soulmates, I have become the unofficial dean of reincarnation. I welcome the characterization, because *I believe we do reincarnate until we learn our lessons and graduate.* And, as I have repeatedly pointed out, there is considerable historical and clinical evidence that reincarnation is a reality" (*Messages from the Master, Tapping into the Power of Love*, by Brian Weiss, M.D., pp.1-2).

But how did Dr. Weiss, a confirmed skeptic, come to believe in reincarnation? Why would he make such a radical shift from a scientific to a spiritual paradigm if not through what Gurdjieff called "self-initiation into the mysteries of life"? Here, then, is how Dr. Brian L. Weiss was called by the merciful law of divine synchronicity to his destiny of growth, love and service because the natural process of individuation through karma and reincarnation had made him ready to be initiated into the secret way of life: One day in 1980 a twenty-seven year old woman whom he calls Catherine in his book *Many Lives, Many Masters* walked into his office "seeking help for her anxiety, panic attacks, and phobias."

For eighteen months Dr. Weiss tried "conventional methods of therapy to help her overcome her symptoms." When nothing seemed to work, he tried hypnosis believing that the source of her problem lay in early childhood memories, which wasn't the case because one day he hypnotized Catherine and "unwittingly" gave her an open-ended directive that changed the course of his life: "Go back to the time from which your symptoms arise." And Catherine took Dr. Weiss completely by surprise, because instead of going back to her early childhood as he expected, she went back to one of her past lives!

That's how a skeptical psychiatrist became introduced to reincarnation and his destiny of serving humanity through past-life regression therapy...

13. The Fallacy of No Separate Self

If Gurdjieff was wrong in his premise that man is not born with an immortal soul, which I categorically believe he was given the proof of my own *becoming*—my past-life regression to the Body of God where all souls come from; the birth of my reflective self-consciousness in my first primordial human life; my regression to some of my key past lives that helped make sense of my current lifetime; and the birth of my spiritual self in my mother's kitchen one fine summer day while she was kneading bread dough on the kitchen table; plus the practical proof that past-life regressionists have not once to my knowledge come up blank when regressing a client to a past lifetime, indicating that everyone has an individual and autonomous "I" that evolves from one lifetime to the next for the divinely ordained purpose of realizing their divine nature, which Jesus called "the pearl of great price—I am led to ask: *why do so many intelligent people continue to believe that Gurdjieff was right in his premise that man is not born with an immortal soul?*

I've done a lot of research online since I began writing this book, reading websites on Gurdjieff's teaching and relevant books that I ordered from Amazon, and I cannot help but be dismayed by the effect that Gurdjieff's belief that man is not born with an immortal soul continues to have upon seekers looking for answers to life's questions, and I have to ask myself: are these people willfully blind to how life is unfolding, or are they simply stubborn?

For years they've had programs on television of psychics communicating with the spirit of dead people, programs like *Crossing Over with John Edwards*, and not long ago I came upon a TV program called *Ghost Inside My Child*, which is all about children remembering their past lives; are Gurdjieffian followers not aware of the emerging spiritual culture, or do they find some clever way of dismissing what so many people are experiencing?

For years Dr. Eben Alexander, a highly trained neurosurgeon and natural born skeptic who believed that consciousness was an epiphenomenon of the brain had a paradigm-shifting medical experience a thousand times more dramatic than Dr. Brian L. Weiss's experience with Catherine and wrote a book called *Proof of Heaven, A Neurosurgeon's Journey into the Afterlife* that chronicles his out-of-body experience which called him to his destiny of service to life by helping to convince the world that the I-consciousness of our individual self is not a byproduct of our brain but exists independently of our biology; once again, proving Gurdjieff wrong to believe that when our body dies we are nothing more than *"merde."*

I wrote a book called *Do We Have an Immortal Soul?* It was inspired by a dialogue between philosopher Ken Wilber, some of whose books I had read, my favorite being *Grace and Grit*, a biographical account of his wife Treya's five year ordeal with cancer, and Brother Wayne Teasdale, author of *The Mystic Heart, Discovering a Universal Spirituality in World Religions,* which I had read also. These two brilliant thinkers believe that we do not have an autonomous self, an individual soul; they believe that we are points of divine light.

Brother Wayne explained to Wilber that he perceived the self to be a point of divine light. He asked Wilber to imagine a huge board that stood between existence and the Godhead. The board is full of tiny holes, and the light of the Godhead that shines through the holes is who we are. Brother Wayne's exact words that I transcribed from the video were:

"We are little points of light, but we are not autonomous in ourselves. We are that light. Or as Eckhart would say, you are God, he, she, or it (is) God, I am God; but God is not you, he, she, it or they. But that infinite light, we are ontologically that in the deepest part of ourselves. That's all we can be."

I don't disagree with this belief that we are all points of divine light, but I strongly disagree that this is all we can be; this is what I intended to prove with *Do We Have an Immortal Soul?* And I hope to firm up my point of view with this book, because I think it's time that the story of how I found my true self was told because, to quote from "Socrates' Secret," Chapter 29 of *Do We Have an Immortal Soul?*— "I" is the mystery of life. "I" is a miraculous unit of reflective self-consciousness that is aware of its own individuality and separateness from life; and although every "I" is made of the same individuated consciousness of life, each "I", in the words of the Romantic Poet John Keats, 'possesses a bliss peculiar to each one by individual existence.' "I" is who we are. It is our distinct individual *core identity*. Like snowflakes, we are all different but the same; but how do we become different? Better still, how do we even become a distinct, separate "I"?"

My story answers this question; but who will believe it? And does it really matter if anyone believes it or not? Perhaps I should answer this question before I continue…

What we believe determines our life. When I was young I was an altar boy, and I believed in heaven and hell. I believed that if I died in a state of mortal sin, I would go to hell; and so, by virtue of my Roman Catholic faith I went to confession whenever I committed a mortal sin so I would be absolved and go to heaven when I died.

My belief in heaven and hell kept me vigilant. I had to watch my behavior, like eating meat on Friday which was a mortal sin. But in its infinite wisdom, the Holy Mother Church decided that it would no longer be a mortal sin to eat meat on Friday; and with one Holy Decree the dreaded fear of eating meat on Friday was removed from my belief system.

The same thing happened with Sunday Mass. Missing Sunday Mass was a mortal sin, but in its infinite wisdom the Holy Mother Church decided that we could attend Mass Saturday evening so we could have Sunday free, and with another holy stroke of the papal pen missing Sunday Mass was no longer a mortal sin; but, of course, one had to attend Saturday evening mass if they wanted Sunday free. And once again, my faith was changed; and as my faith changed, so did the belief that determined me. And so it goes with life.

As our faith changes, so does our life. And as our beliefs change, so does our life. This is why I find it curious that so many followers of Gurdjieff's teaching continue to believe that man is not born with an immortal soul in light of all the evidence that our self-identity, our autonomous individual self, can and does exist independent of our biology.

True, there is no hard scientific proof yet (and I doubt there will ever be for intractable skeptics like Richard Dawkins, author of

The God Delusion); but then, neither is Gurdjieff's belief based upon hard scientific evidence. So the point I want to make is that our beliefs determine our life, and if we don't believe that we are born with an autonomous, individual soul like the brilliant philosopher Ken Wilber and Brother Wayne Teasdale and every faithful Buddhist and atheist on this planet, our life is going to be predetermined by our belief and all that subsequently follows, like the lady who wanted to believe that she did not have a separate self and lived in unbearable anguish that her belief was not strong enough.

She was in tears when she confessed her lack of belief to her spiritual teacher Francis Lucille in the online video that I saw, and so moved was I by her tears that I felt compelled to resolve her dilemma which was born of the misperception that we do not have a separate and autonomous individual self, because I knew that understanding the reality of her *becoming* would heal her of the pain she felt from the teleological thrust of her need to be her true self and her desperate need to believe that she did not have a separate self.

In my spiritual healing sessions with St. Padre Pio, which became the basis of my novel *Healing with Padre Pio,* he told me that **spiritual healing comes with understanding**; and I felt obliged by the imperative of my initiation into the mysteries of our *becoming* to offer a way out of this poor woman's dilemma—her, and the millions of souls trapped in the mental prison of their belief that we do not have a separate self, a treacherous belief that impedes the individuation process to wholeness and completeness of one's divine, true self.

But before I explain the reason for that heart-wrenching exchange between the spiritual teacher of nonduality Francis Lucille and the innocent devotee who wanted desperately to believe that she did not have a separate self, let me relate how I made the simple but phenomenal discovery that resolved the dilemma of our *becoming* through the consciousness of our *being* and *non-being* while I was "working" on myself with Gurdjieff's teaching.

It started with my simple dream of two successful Hollywood movie directors. In my dream, these directors were good friends professionally, but personally they were complete opposites and couldn't stand each other. One was centered in his *non-being* (his archetypal shadow self), and the other was centered in his *being* (his authentic self), and they revealed their type by their character; their interests, manners, speech, and behavior.

One was difficult and impossible to please. Nothing was ever good enough for him, and he made life very difficult for everyone on his set; but he made great movies. The other was no less demanding, but in a completely different way. He was kind, understanding, and very generous with everyone on his set; and he also made great movies.

I had no idea what this dream meant at first; but then I remembered reading something in *The Teachers of Gurdjieff*, by Rafael Lefort. This story is probably allegory, because as J. G. Bennett surmised in his book *Gurdjieff: Making a New World*, he doubted that any of Gurdjieff's teachers were still alive when Lefort went on his quest for Gurdjieff's teachers. Nonetheless, one aged Sufi Master who said he taught Gurdjieff implied to Rafael Lefort that there were two paths in life: one by way of *being*, and the other by way of *non-being*; and this resonated with me instantly, because I knew that mine was the path of *non-being*—which many years later I explored in my memoir *The Summoning of Noman*.

But what did this Sufi Master mean by the two paths of *being* and *non-being*? Don't we individuate in our own identity by way of both *being* and *non-being*? Isn't this the reality of our ego/shadow personality? We grow in our identity through our relationship with life both consciously (our ego personality) and unconsciously (our shadow self), because through our interactions with life we take in the life force that nourishes our individuating Soul self, as I came to reason out with my own journey to my true self; so what does it mean to take the path of *being* or the path of *non-being*? How can these paths be separate? Or are they?

Despite the fact that I knew in my heart that I was on the path of *non-being*, I could not explain what that meant; I just knew that I was centered in my false self when I went on my quest for my true self, which I intimately related in *The Summoning of Noman*. Suffice to say here that I finally did become aware of what that venerable Sufi Master meant by his comment to Rafael Lefort: "Real People have experienced *being* and *non-being* and have long ago entered a stage of evolution when neither state means anything to them" (*The Teachers of Gurdjieff*, Rafael Lefort, p. 96-7, italics mine).

This is the same state of evolution that I experienced when I made the two into one by "working" on myself with Gurdjieff's teaching, my *Royal Dictum,* and the sayings of Jesus and transcended myself; and in my new state of consciousness I could say: **I am what I am not, and I am not what I am; I am both, but neither: I am Soul.**

And it was from this state of transcended consciousness that I explored the paths of *being* and *non-being* in the life of my high school hero and literary mentor Ernest Hemingway and the life of Carl Gustav Jung in my literary memoir *The Lion that Swallowed Hemingway*, with Hemingway taking the path of *non-being* and Jung taking the path of *being*; and the conclusion that I came to was that one's life story, to borrow Jung's metaphor for the individuation of one's Soul self, can get stuck in either path and fail to transcend itself.

This was the simple but phenomenal discovery that I made about the individuation process that Carl Jung wanted to talk to me about when he came to me in my dream after reading my book *The Way of Soul*, which was published on the Other Side but not out here (and it still isn't, for that matter); my realization that our individuating Soul self can be centered in either the *being* or *non-being* state of our *becoming.*

In the paradoxical language of our *becoming,* this means that we are what we are not and we are not what we are; we are both our ego and shadow selves. Our ego is our *being* self, and our shadow is our *non-being* self; and through the dynamic interplay of our ego and shadow we *become* and grow in the identity of our Soul self until the natural process of individuation through karma and reincarnation can take us no further and we have to take evolution into our own hands to make the two into one, as I did one day in my mother's kitchen, and by this I simply mean that I gave birth to my spiritual self, to use Christ's metaphor—or, if you will, I experienced that moment of spiritual self-realization when I transcended the consciousness of my *being* and *non-being* and *became* my true self.

But what does it mean to be centered in either our *being* or *non-being* self? This is the mystery that I set out to solve when I went on my quest for my true self after I had that sexual experience that brutally shocked my conscience awake. I knew that the person who did what he did that night was me but not me, and I had to find an answer to this mystery; and I divested my business interests and went to France to begin my quest for my true self. And when I returned to Canada I went to university to study philosophy, and I discovered Gurdjieff; and with his teaching of "work" on myself the secret way of life opened up to me and I found my true self by *becoming* my true self, and I resolved the paradox of our *being* and *non-being*.

These states of consciousness of *being* and *non-being* are so vast they can trap our individuating soul self from one lifetime to the next, if not for eternity; and only by the grace of God can we make the two into one and transcend the *I Am* consciousness of *being* and *non-being* and realize the individuated consciousness of our Soul self—because the consciousness of *I Am* is the pure consciousness of our *being* and *non-being* selves and not the transcendent consciousness of our separate Soul self, which is both *being* and *non-being* but neither.

This is why I've always had an uneasy feeling about Buddhism. As attracted as I was to the ethics of this spiritual path and the life of the Dalai Lama whose books I read and studied, I was very uneasy about its belief that we do not have an autonomous self, and I never pursued this path any further. I did practice TM (Transcendental Meditation) for several years, but I finally abandoned it for the active life of Gurdjieff's teaching of "work on oneself," because in this path I saw the immediate efficacy of my own *becoming*. My own mother even said to me one day, "You change before my very eyes."

I changed before her eyes because I was transforming my consciousness, which was deeply grounded in my family shadow that had a hold upon my psyche. Suffice to say for now that I felt uneasy about the Buddhist belief that we don't have an individual soul, and the most that I could get out of this teaching was to liberate myself from my ego personality which Buddhism declared to be my ephemeral and illusory self; but every instinct in me resisted the notion that I did not have an individual separate self, because I knew deep in my soul that I was real.

That's why I was attracted to Gurdjieff's teaching despite his belief that man is not born with an immortal soul; because with his teaching I could "create" my own soul, which was vastly different from the Buddhist notion of the non-self of pure awareness. The very idea of being a non-self so repulsed me that I could not fathom how so many people throughout the centuries could buy into it, but they did and continue to do so; but not without consequence, as the lady who cried in anguish when she told her spiritual teacher that she wanted to believe that she was not a separate self from the *I Am* consciousness of pure *being* and *non-being* and despaired her lack of faith in his teaching of non-duality.

    Many writers on Gurdjieff's life believe that he was influenced by Buddhism, and I have no doubt that he was because he travelled to the Far East in search of hidden knowledge on the real nature of man which he knew existed in underground mystery schools, and he was by nature an eclectic who took the best from each teaching that he studied and poured it into his Fourth Way teaching; but because he called his teaching "esoteric Christianity," I knew that he had learned Christ's secret of making the two into one—meaning, he had learned the secret of the mystical marriage of our two selves, the self of our *being* and the self of our *non-being*, which created a third transcended self that he called our immortal soul. So it's very likely that Gurdjieff was influenced by the Buddhist notion of the non-self, but like myself he could not accept that this was all there was to life; there had to be more, and he found it in esoteric Christianity which taught the secret of how to "create" our own soul.

    Ironically, as my own journey of self-discovery has proven (at least for myself if not for anyone else), we do not have to create our own soul because we are all immortal souls in the process of realizing our immortal nature through karma and reincarnation, and Gurdjieff's teaching, like Christ's teaching, merely facilitates the process with *conscious effort* and *intentional suffering*. But, as I said, because our beliefs affect our life, Gurdjieff's belief that we do not have an immortal soul can seriously impede one's life story, as it has for many disillusioned followers of his teaching, just as it has for followers of Buddhism who believe that they do not have a separate self and are forever at odds with their natural evolutionary impulse to become their true, divine self. Their belief impedes their *becoming*.

    I have addressed this issue in my book *Stupidity Is Not a Gift of God*, in my essay "On the Evolutionary Impulse to Individuate: A Response to the Spiritual Path of Evolutionary Enlightenment," so I need not expound upon it any further; suffice to say that despite Gurdjieff's belief that man is not born with an immortal soul, which I suspect was the influence that Buddhism had upon him, he discovered the secret of how to individuate the *I Am* consciousness of our *being* and *non-being* and "create" our own immortal soul. This is why Gurdjieff appeals to so many people, because he gives them a sense of hope that appeals to the longing in one's soul to be all that they are destined to be, their true self.

14. When the Fat Lady Stops Singing

It's hard to admit to oneself that one has been taken for a fool by life and walk away from their experience without rancor; and if one does walk away, who would want to talk about their humiliation? No one wants to be seen as a fool. But that's how the game of life is played by the Archetypal Shadow, the arch deceiver of humanity that has the power of propriety to keep us quiet about our humiliations and flawed heroes. In all honesty however, I could not throw the baby out with the bathwater when the fat lady stopped singing; and I overcame my humiliation by writing a spiritual musing for my blog on my experience with a New Age spiritual teaching when I discovered that the man I admired and respected had founded his teaching upon a fraudulent foundation and played us all for fools:—

Parable of the Packages

"By indirections find directions out."
Hamlet Act 2, Scene 1
Shakespeare

Truth comes in many packages, and no two packages are the same. Some packages are plain and simple, covered in brown paper and tied with plain white string, and others are wrapped in gold or silver paper and tied with elaborate ribbons of many colours; but the truth inside the packages is all the same. This is my parable of the packages, and today's spiritual musing...

I became a truth seeker from the day I read Somerset Maugham's novel *The Razor's Edge* in high school. That was a lifetime ago. Recently I was online doing research on the alluring New Age spiritual teaching of the Light and Sound of God that I embraced for many years when I came to the end of my study of another teaching that had opened up the secret way of life to me, Gurdjieff's enigmatic Fourth Way teaching, and I chanced upon the movie *The Razor's Edge* online and had to watch it again just to see how far I had come in my long journey of self-discovery.

I had a heavy heart from my disconcerting research on the inveterate truth-seeking founder of the teaching that had come to me serendipitously to expand my spiritual horizons when I had to move on from Gurdjieff's teaching founded upon the premise that we are not born with an immortal soul but can create one with *conscious effort* and *intentional suffering*, because Gurdjieff's teaching of "work on oneself" had done all it could for me; and I watched *The Razor's Edge* with such fierce objectivity that it made Maugham's hero Larry Darrell's quest for truth seem almost shallow and frivolous, but I enjoyed it all the same because it brought back many memories.

I had seen the movie long ago on television, the Tyrone Power version and not the Bill Murray fiasco that missed the point of the whole story; but after all these many years and my online research on the origin of Maugham's hero Larry Darrell I came away from the story skeptical of the author's literary intentions, which I now saw as aesthetic pretentions not unlike those of the founder of the New Age spiritual teaching who was not what he purported to be. He was a real person who fabricated a fictional spiritual identity, while Larry Darrell was a fictional composite whom Maugham had fabricated out of his own seeker self and people that he knew: two separate packages with their own truth that in my profound naiveté I bought into respectively.

Larry Darrell was the central character of *The Razor's Edge*, and he walked away from his fiancé and conventional life to go out into the world to seek an answer to the meaning and purpose of life. He was still a young man with his whole life ahead of him, but he had an experience during the war that called him to a higher purpose than marriage and family life, and he was bound by his own conscience to be true to his calling. Larry was a fighter pilot in WWI, and during a "dogfight" in the air his pilot friend sacrificed his life to save Larry's; and Larry had to know why he was spared and his friend had to die. That's why he became a truth seeker whose story the famous author William Somerset Maugham had to write; but it's in the way that he packaged Larry's story that interested me all these many years later.

When I read *The Razor's Edge* in high school I took Maugham at his word that his story was true. "I have invented nothing," he tells us early in the story; and I even made inquiries through a magazine advertisement with an agency that hunted down lost books to see if they could locate for me the book that Maugham's fictional hero Larry Darrell had written (which only revealed my incredible naiveté to my English teacher who had assigned the novel for us to read); but Maugham gave his novel such credibility by inserting himself into the story that I foolishly believed his story to be biographically true. As he said, "I have invented nothing."

That's how clever the author was in his packaging of Larry Darrell's care-free bohemian life and romantic quest for truth, but he was not half as clever as the modern day founder of the New Age spiritual teachings of the Light and Sound of God that I lived for over thirty years; this fearless truth-seeking American writer with a charming southern accent invented a whole new ancient lineage of Spiritual Masters and packaged his own life and teaching with a highly seductive but fraudulent mythology that gave innocent seekers like myself what we were looking for, and much more. Which begs the question: *does packaging damage the truth inside the package?*

I was born into a southern Italian Roman Catholic family, and I embraced the packaging of my Roman Catholic faith without question. I was an altar boy, and I even considered becoming a priest one day; but all through high school I suffered from what can only be called spiritual claustrophobia because my faith constrained me, and when I read *The Razor's Edge* in high school I was called to a higher purpose and became a truth seeker like my hero Larry Darrell. And I also discovered reincarnation.

First in my dreams with four past-life recollection dreams of living in another body in another time, and later in Plato's Dialogues and the Edgar Cayce literature and many other books; and I walked away from my Roman Catholic faith which I learned many years later was a beautifully wrapped package of the true teachings of the secret way that Jesus gave to the world in his cryptic sayings and parables; but it took many years before I resolved my issues with my Roman Catholic faith and Jesus Christ's true teaching, which I expounded upon in my novel *Healing with Padre Pio*.

If reincarnation is a fact of life, as I came to believe, then our immortal soul is not created at the moment of our human conception as Christianity would have us believe; we pre-exist our mortal human body and return to live life over again and again to grow in our divine nature until we have grown enough to break the recurring cycle of life and death and are called to a higher purpose, like my fictional hero Larry Darrell and all truth seekers who are called by their destiny; but does this make the enticing Christian package of Christ's death upon the cross for our salvation moot?

At first I thought it did, until I explored the contents of the package and learned the true meaning of Christ's teaching; and I ceased to harbor resentment for my Roman Catholic faith that denied me the truth of the secret way of life found in the sayings and parables of Jesus inside the package, because my Roman Catholic faith had instilled in me a conscience and fine sense of moral purpose, and inside the packaged lie of Christianity can be found the sacred truth of our divine nature.

So I was well prepared for what I learned about the clever founder of the New Age spiritual teaching that I embraced without question for the better part of thirty years, and I harbor no resentment for the man and his packaged teaching as many members who walked away from it have because they were disillusioned by the monumental lies that he had perpetrated upon his gullible followers.

The founder of this New Age spiritual teaching has been proven to be a clever fabricator who embroidered a mythical story which he plagiarized from authentic spiritual sources, a story so brilliantly woven that it took the innocence of an intrepid twenty year-old graduate student doing research for a term paper to discover the false coins that this man had mingled with the true inside the golden papered package of his spiritual teaching that he released to the world in the soul-searching, flower-powered 1960s; but rather than come clean with its fraudulent history, the current leader of this teaching continues to cling to the embroidered story brazenly perpetrated by its fraudulent myth-making founder, and this mars the package with an ugly stain that gravely impairs the spiritual integrity of this New Age spiritual teaching of the Light and Sound of God, so much so that I had to leave.

The fat lady stopped singing, and I walked away from this teaching when I finished writing *The Pearl of Great Price* which set my feet firmly upon my own path, and I comforted myself with Karen Blixen's insight that *art is the truth above the facts of life*, because I finally understood why the great artificer William Somerset Maugham, who besides fanning the flame of my calling to become a truth seeker also revealed to me an unteachable secret on the art of story writing, did what he did to get to the truth of his story above the facts of his fictional hero Larry Darrell's life and why the clever founder of this New Age spiritual teaching of the Light and Sound of God fabricated his spellbinding story to bring the true coins of ancient spiritual teachings *(the truth above the facts of life)* to a spiritually famished world, and in the process made a comfortable living for his self-serving efforts; both my fictional truth-seeking hero Larry Darrell and the fraudulent mythmaking writer and his spiritually seductive New Age teaching gave me what I needed for my journey to wholeness and completeness; and as bittersweet as it may be, this is my parable of the packages, and I hold no grudge for these arch deceivers who played me for a fool because this is what I needed to get to where I have to be in my own path to fulfillment.

As difficult as this spiritual musing was to write, I had to have it on record for the strange story of my parallel life; because it taught me one of the most difficult lessons that a truth seeker can ever learn—that all paths to God, whether true or false, are necessary for one's spiritual growth; for how is one to know about his *non-being* if he does not experience the inauthentic in his journey to wholeness and completeness?

That's what the New Age spiritual teaching of the Light and Sound of God did for me by concentrating the false in me to such a point that I could no longer suffer the indignity of my own inauthenticity and had to have a spiritual healing with St. Padre Pio, which I wrote about in my novel *Healing with Padre Pio;* and although it will take time to get over the hurt of being taken for a fool by this New Age teaching, I am free of the subconscious hold it had upon my psyche and can live my own life now in the fullness of my wholeness.

15. Becoming Spiritually Literate

When I came back from France I went to university to study philosophy because I thought that the mother of all disciplines (etymologically, philosophy means love of wisdom) would help me find an answer to the haunting questions of my life, *who am I?* and *why am I?* I was looking for my true self, but all I got from philosophy was chatter; brilliant, but chatter nonetheless, and my fate pulled me away to look for another path.

Now that I have the luxury of having found my true self, as I tell this strange story of my lonely quest of self-discovery I can't help but feel that our life is choreographed; because in all honesty, I now believe the only reason I was called to university was to find Gurdjieff's teaching of "work on oneself" which awakened me to the secret way of life.

The secret way of life is not a spiritual path, as such; it is the inherent wisdom of life that we take in with every experience we have, and the more we experience life the more life wisdom we will take in. I needed a lot of wisdom to answer my haunting questions, and Gurdjieff's teaching of "work on oneself" taught me how to get the most wisdom out of life.

I began my philosophy studies at university with enormous, if not sycophantic respect for the great thinkers of the world; and every time I was introduced to a new philosopher I was excited by what I might find. But one by one, they all disappointed me; and then one day I felt myself drifting aimlessly in an open sea of endless speculation, and I panicked.

I had found Gurdjieff by this time, and my unconscious had manifested the mandala of the squaring of the circle in the darkness of my bedroom; so my fate was sealed, and it was only a matter of time before the ineluctable forces of my fate severed me from academia, because philosophy had served its purpose of attracting Gurdjieff into my life.

True, I may have found Gurdjieff's teaching had I not gone to university; but I've grown to understand that one has to be in the right place at the right time to get what they need to continue on their journey to wholeness and completeness; that's why I've come to believe that **our life is choreographed by the mysterious forces of our destiny.**

This, of course, is the mystery of our *becoming*; because we are free to choose the life we live, as I did by choosing to go to university; but, paradoxically, the life we live also chooses us because it's what we need to serve our destined purpose, as Gurdjieff's teaching which I found at university served my purpose of finding my true self.

But, believe me, it nearly drove me mad trying to resolve the paradox of our free will and destined purpose; and I would never have done so had I not made a personal vow when I dropped out of university to build my life upon the truth of my own experiences and not the truth of others—regardless of who they were, however brilliant or revered and respected; and the more trust I placed in the simple truths of my own experiences, the more the secret way of life opened up to me, until one day I began to "see" and "hear" life speak to me.

But this did not just "happen" to me as I went about my daily life, it came about by the efforts that I made to create the right conditions for life to speak to me; like practicing Gurdjieff's techniques of *self-remembering, non-identifying, conscious effort,* and *intentional suffering*, and living my *Royal Dictum* and the sayings of Jesus. In effect, I sensitized myself to life with the concentrated intensity of my experiences and became spiritually literate.

Although I had found Gurdjieff's teaching and "worked" on myself with conscious effort, I never stopped looking for other ways to find my true self; and I read enormously, starting with all the books on Gurdjieff that I could get from *Samuel Weiser* in New York City, and every book that called out to me as I scoured all the bookstores in Thunder Bay where I went to pick up supplies for my painting business, books written by other seekers like Carlos Castaneda who introduced the world to a "man of knowledge" called Don Juan, *Seth Speaks, The Eternal Validity of the Soul* by Jan Roberts, James Redfield's *The Celestine Prophecy,* Caroline Myss's *Anatomy of the Spirit*, Idries Shaw's *The Sufis, The Seven Storey Mountain* by the Trappist monk and prolific writer Thomas Merton and numerous books of an eclectic spiritual nature until I had amassed a personal library of thousands of books.

Each book I read was another person's life wisdom expressed in the language of their own path or discipline, like separate windows onto the soul of life; and if what they had to say spoke to me, I added it to my own belief system—but always with the understanding that life would eventually prove to me whether another person's truth was true or false, as it did with an offshoot Christian solar cult teaching that did irreparable damage to my eyesight and also with the spiritual path of the Light and Sound of God once it had served its purpose.

There's always a price to pay when one becomes a seeker; that's why Carl Jung told Miguel Serrano in *C. G. Jung and Hermann Hesse, A Record of Two Friendships* that "the path is very difficult." No one comes away unscathed, and more often than not one does not come away at all and stays on a path they have outgrown but can't break away from for one reason or another, like one of my customers whose house I painted every few years who always told me that she got nothing out of her religion but went to church for the company; but she was a good person who was blessed with some measure of spiritual literacy.

In fact, among the many books that I loaned her over the years was *Spiritual Literacy, Reading the Sacred in Everyday Life*, by Frederic and Mary Ann Brussat, the only book that I had found that specifically addressed the mystery of the secret way of life that is the essential nature of the life experience. "Life is a sacred adventure," the authors write in the Introduction. "Every day we encounter signs that point to the active presence of Spirit in the world around us." And, they add, "Spiritual literacy is practiced in all the world's wisdom traditions. Medieval Catholic monks called it 'reading the book of the world.'"

"'The spiritual life is, at root, a matter of seeing,'" John Shea, a contemporary Catholic theologian, reminds us. 'It is all of life seen from a certain perspective. It is waking, sleeping, dreaming, eating, drinking, working, loving, relaxing, recreating, walking, sitting, standing, and breathing...spirit suffuses everything; and so the spiritual life is simply life, wherever and whatever, seen from the vantage point of spirit,'" (*Spiritual Literacy: Reading the Sacred in Everyday Life*, p. 28).

Life has its own language that speaks to us every moment of the day, but we cannot hear what it has to tell us if we don't pay attention; that's what "work" on myself taught me how to do. The more I "worked" on myself, the more sensitive I became to the Voice of Divine Spirit that spoke to me in the silent language of the secret way; but this is a deep, deep mystery that needs my full attention to give proper context to my strange story.

Being a writer, I've learned a thing or two about how the creative process works; and the best way to convey the deep mysteries of life is by way of images, symbols, and analogy because discursive explanations always fall short of what we want to say; and the image that comes to mind as I try to explain the secret way is that of an invisible benevolent teacher/guide who walks alongside us every single moment of our day, whispering into our ear whatever we need to know to show us the way to wholeness and completeness.

The irony of course is that this is the way life really works, because Divine Spirit is the ground of all being and silent voice of the secret way; but it takes a lot of serious life experience to awaken to this mystery, and that's what "work" on myself did for me as I transformed the consciousness of my *being* and *non-being* and transcended myself until I saw life from a spiritual perspective, and by serious life experience I mean experiences that we have at great personal risk which Robert Frost epitomized in "The Road Not Taken."

Experience is fraught with meaning, which is why my high school hero and literary mentor Ernest Hemingway went out of his way to experience as much life as he could so he would have something meaningful to write about; and in the process wrote some of the best stories ever written, like *The Old Man and the Sea* and my favorite Hemingway story *The Snows of Kilimanjaro*, and his memoir *A Moveable Feast* which brought tears to my eyes.

"The more he learns from experience the more truly he can imagine," said Hemingway to a young writer he called "Mice" in the October 1933 *Esquire* article "Monologue to the Maestro: A High Seas Letter," adding invaluable advice that I took to heart, as I did anything that Hemingway had to say about story writing: "Good writing is true writing. If a man is making a story up it will be true in proportion to the amount of knowledge of life that he has and how conscientious he is; so that if he makes something up it is as it would truly be" (*By-Line: Ernest Hemingway*, p. 187).

Which is why the great writer said to me in a dream one night while I was living in Annecy, France where I had gone to begin my quest for my true self and work on my first novel, which I called *This Petty Pace*, taken from Hamlet's famous "to be or not to be" soliloquy, "I have pissed out more life than you have lived."

That hurt, because he was my high school hero; but today, all of these many years later, especially after all the reading that I did for my literary memoir *The Lion that Swallowed Hemingway*, I know precisely what he meant by his insensitive comment that he had pissed out more life than I had lived: **the truth of life comes from experience.**

Although I was only twenty-three when Hemingway visited me in my dream, by the same age he had already been wounded in the war, fallen in love with his nurse Agnes von Kurowsky whom he later immortalized as Catherine Barkley in his novel *A Farewell to Arms*, and had experienced enough life to write dozens of stories, which he did in his Nick Adams series and other stories drawn upon his life-packed youth; so I had no right to take offense. I was still green behind the ears, and it would take a long time before I learned the great writer's secret which he expressed in his advice to his friend F. Scott Fitzgerald: "Forget your personal tragedy. We are all bitched from the start and you especially have to be hurt like hell before you can write seriously. But when you get the damned hurt use it—don't cheat with it. Be as faithful to it as a scientist—but don't think anything is of any importance because it happens to you or anyone belonging to you" (to F. Scott Fitzgerald, 1934, *Selected Letters*, p. 408).

Hemingway was obsessed with truth in his stories, which is why he said that he always began his stories with "one true sentence," upon which he built the rest of his story; but truth never comes cheaply, especially the great truths of life.

It cost me over thirty thousand dollars, lifelong insomnia, and my long distance running habit which I looked forward to every single day, to learn my lesson on karma when a contract that I had to hang drywall and tape and paint seven new houses on the native reserve near my hometown went sour on me; I suffered unbearable anguish on that job, and all because I had to assume responsibility for my job going wrong. Here's the karmic lesson that I learned: being the contractor of the job, I was responsible for all the drywall hanging deficiencies that my crew made, which cost me extra time and money; and being the contractor of the job, I was responsible for all the taping deficiencies that my crew made, which again cost me extra time and money; and being the contractor of the job, I was responsible for all the painting deficiencies that my crew made, which again cost me extra time and money.

All of these deficiencies were pointed out to me by the building inspector (agent of karma) who came from Thunder Bay to check out each phase of the building project, and because all of these deficiencies took up extra time my contract ran over the limit that I was allowed to complete my contract and I had to pay a one hundred dollar fine for every day over the limit. In total, my contract ended up costing me over thirty thousand dollars, and I never made a cent. In fact, I went in the hole so much that it took years to make up for what I lost.

So what did I learn about karma? I was the contractor, so I was the principal agent responsible for hanging the drywall, taping, and painting. So the hanging deficiencies were passed on to the taper, which was me; the taping deficiencies were passed on to the painter, which was me; and the painting deficiencies were passed on to me also; and **the bitter truth that I learned about karma is that the buck stopped with me!** In other words, karma simply means that we pass on to ourselves our own deficiencies; and one day we will have to pay for them, if not in this lifetime, definitely another because this is how life works.

But I've never written a story about my experience on the reserve, because it's still too emotional to think about, as are some of my other very personal and private experiences like the accidental awakening of the Kundalini and my solar cult misadventure that damaged my eyesight; that's why I admire Hemingway, because he had the courage to write about his hurt despite the fact that most of it was of his own doing, like betraying his first wife Hadley Richardson, the one true love of his life whom he gladly would not have betrayed by having an affair with their friend Pauline Pfeiffer had he the chance to do it all over again, which he confessed to in what one day may be seen as the one of the most tragic lines in all of literature: "When I saw my wife again standing by the tracks as the train came in by the piled logs at the station, I wish I had died before I ever loved anyone but her" (*A Moveable Feast*, p.208).

That's the pain and sorrow of regret, which I explored in my novel *The Golden Seed* in which I have a disillusioned man revisit the decision he made to have an affair with the woman who broke up his marriage and destroyed his family; but that's fiction. Or is it?

This is what makes my story so strange, because if I'm to take St. Padre Pio at his word, and I do, I came back to relive my same life over again to achieve a different outcome, which I explored in my memoir *The Summoning of Noman*; so what can we make of this?

To be quite honest, I'm still bewildered by the whole experience, despite exploring my parallel life through my dreams in *The Summoning of Noman*; but my objective in this story is to honor Gurdjieff for his teaching and correct his misperception that man is not born with an immortal soul, which the strange story of my own life has proven.

16. Cathedral of My Past Lives

As I said, when I dropped out of university to forge my own path with Gurdjieff's teaching, I vowed to build my life upon the truth of my own experiences; but some of my experiences were so "out there" that I could not share them with anyone, nor even write about them. But because they were mine, they became the truth that I built my life upon; that's how I came to my understanding of the Three Circles of Life—the exoteric, mesoteric, and esoteric stages of evolution. And it all started with my past-life regressions.

Because life is an individual journey, we never get the answers we need until we are ready for them—despite how desperately we may want them. This was one of the hardest truths of my life to come to, because I desperately needed to know who I was. Little did I realize however that to know who I was, I had to *become* who I was; which meant that **I had to grow in the consciousness of my true self to realize my true self**.

This was my dilemma, which the omniscient guiding forces of my destiny resolved by inspiring me to go to university where I "chanced" upon Gurdjieff's teaching that impelled me to create my *Royal Dictum* which awakened me to the secret way of life; and by living the secret way I inadvertently made the two into one (my *being* and *non-being*) and realized my true self that glorious summer day in my mother's kitchen while she was kneading bread dough on the kitchen table. And this made me ready for the deep mystery of life.

The deep mystery of life is the Divine Plan of God. Now that I had *become* my true self, I knew that I was Soul, the individualized consciousness of my *being* and *non-being*; but I did not know WHERE I came from, WHY I was, and WHERE I was going. But because I had *become* my true self, I was ready for the answers; and life presented me with the opportunity to find them when Penny and I relocated to Georgian Bay.

By happenstance, I met a past-life regressionist one day at our first satsang class at the home of one of the members of our new spiritual community in Orillia, just north of our home in Bluewater,

Gurdjieff Was Wrong But His Teaching Works

Georgian Bay. She was a reflexologist who also did past-life regressions, and I got her business card because I knew from the day I read Jess Stearn's book *The Search for the Soul: Psychic Lives of Taylor Caldwell* that I would one day write a book on my own past lives; so I made arrangements with this lady and had seven past-life regressions, which became the basis of my novel *Cathedral of My Past Lives*.

For literary reasons, I chose to write a novel instead of a straight autobiographical account of my regressions because I had learned from Hemingway that I could never do justice to my experience without invoking the "magic dust" of my imagination.

After he wrote a straight autobiographical account of his African safari in *Green Hills of Africa*, Hemingway learned the hard way when his book failed to meet the aesthetic requirements of a great story that the "magic dust" of imagination enhances the truth of a story and makes it more real than the real thing; which is precisely what the author of *Out of Africa* Karen Blixen meant when she said, "Art is the truth above the facts of life." But this requires an explanation before I continue with my story.

In a letter to Bernard Berenson, Hemingway wrote: "You know that fiction, prose rather, is possibly the roughest trade of all in writing. You do not have the reference, the old important reference. You have the sheet of blank paper, the pencil, and the obligation to invent truer than things can be true. You have to take what is not palpable and make it completely palpable and also make it seem normal and so that it can become a part of the experience of the person who reads it" (to Bernard Berenson, 1954, *Selected Letters*, p. 837).

I knew that my seven past-life regressions would not be palpable to the average reader, or perhaps any reader for that matter; because not only were the past lives that I was regressed to extreme to the point of incredulity, one in particular was so extreme that no one in their right mind would believe it; and my job as a writer was to make my experience palpable.

But how? My fourth past-life regression was so incredible that the only thing I could do was to abandon to my creative unconscious; and I wrote and simply let the story tell itself, which every creative writer learns to do when they are working on a novel. This is what makes creative writing so magical that writers like Norman Mailer call it "spooky," because the creative unconscious can take the facts of life and transform them into a story that is more true than true, if one can possibly imagine such a creature.

This is what Adrienne Rich meant when she said, "poetry (prose as well) is an act of the imagination that transforms reality into a deeper perception of what is." The "magic dust" of imagination transforms the truth of our life into a deeper perception of that truth; which is merely another way of saying that **art magnifies the truth of life**. And my past-life regressions, especially my regression to the Body of God, magnified the truth of the reincarnational process of Soul's evolution through life. This is why art is so vitally important to our culture, because it helps us to understand life.

I was compelled by my need to know WHO I was, which I resolved by living the secret way of life, and my need to know WHY I was and WHERE I came from and WHERE I was going eventually attracted me to a past-life regressionist in Orillia who provided me with the opportunity to satisfy my need to know; and that's what the "spooky" process of my creative unconscious answered with my novel memoir *Cathedral of My Past Lives*.

It's not published yet, but the magnified truth of my experience gave birth to the Divine Plan of God, which resolved the longing in my soul to know the meaning and purpose of life that my creative unconscious worked out in the Three Circles of Life.

Here, then, is the truth above the facts of my life that *Cathedral of My Past Lives* gave birth to; but first, let me relate how the title of my novel was revealed to me, because this adds a little more spice to the strangeness of my story.

This also happened in Orillia. Another member of our spiritual community was born with a psychic gift, and when I told her about the novel I had just written on my past-life regressions she instantly saw a vision of my novel with an image of a magnificent cathedral and the title *Cathedral of My Past Lives* and my name on the cover; but it took several years before the image of the cathedral revealed itself to me as the throne, or divine truth of Soul's evolution through the three stages of life as I had experienced them; and this is how the Divine Plan of God became my truth above the facts of my life.

The image of the cathedral symbolizes the holy truth of God's Divine Plan, the church of Soul's purpose in life which is to come from the Body of God as an un-self-realized atom of God and evolve through the exoteric, mesoteric, and esoteric stages of life and return to God a fully self-realized Soul, as the evolution of my own life exemplified.

My own life symbolizes the archetypal pattern of Soul's journey from God, through life, and back to God which is why my book was called *Cathedral of My Past Lives*; and that's what made it so incredible and next to impossible to make palpable.

Here then is the truth above the facts of my life that my creative unconscious worked out: we all come from God as atoms of God's Body, but we do not have reflective self-consciousness. We have consciousness, but no self-conscious; and our purpose in life is to create a new "I" of God. **Giving birth to a new "I" of God is the purpose of life**, and each atom of God evolves through the three stages of life to realize its divine nature. These stages are the exoteric, mesoteric, and esoteric stages of evolution.

The exoteric stage of evolution is the first stage where the atom of God evolves through the lowest life form on up to a life form that will constellate enough *life force*, which as I experienced is the *I Am* consciousness of Soul, to give birth to a new "I" of God, just as I experienced in my fourth past life regression when I had the dawning of my reflective self-consciousness in my first primordial human lifetime as the alpha male of a group of ten or twelve higher primates.

This was an incredible experience. I *actually* experienced the birth of my own reflective self-consciousness in my regression. It was a rudimentary sense of self, but there was no mistaking that I had separated from my group consciousness with the dawning of my reflective self, because I now experienced my own separateness; and this threw me into confusion which lasted for the rest of my life—and many lifetimes to come.

Making sense of my separateness was what my evolution through the exoteric first stage of evolution was all about, and with each new life that I lived I grew and evolved in my reflective self-consciousness until I had evolved enough to question my reason for being, which I did in my lifetime as a student of Pythagoras in ancient

Greece, thus beginning my evolution through the mesoteric second stage of evolution.

The exoteric stage of evolution had taken me as far as it could take me and I was pulled into the second stage. The exoteric first stage is governed by the immutable law of karma, and not until one is evolved enough to realize that karma is a personal responsibility will one be ready for the mesoteric stage of evolution where one learns to take karmic responsibility for their own life; and when one has evolved enough in the second stage to find the secret way he will be initiated by life into the mystery of *conscious individuation* and give birth to his spiritual self, as I experienced when I found the secret way with Gurdjieff's teaching.

I could get no more definite proof that Gurdjieff was wrong about man not being born with an immortal soul than my own past-life regressions, because I experienced myself as an immortal atom of God in God's Body where all souls come from and then I experienced the birth of my reflective self-consciousness in my first primordial human lifetime; and with my regressions to my other lifetimes, I connected the dots as I wrote *Cathedral of My Past Lives* and realized that the purpose of life is to evolve the "I" of God until we become spiritual self-realized souls. This is what Carl Jung intimated with his own journey through life:

"Unconscious wholeness therefore seems to me the true *spiritus rector* of all biological and psychic events. Here is a principle which strives for total realization—which in man's case signifies the attainment of total consciousness. Attainment of consciousness is culture in the broadest sense, and self-knowledge is therefore the heart and essence of this process" (*Memories, Dreams, Reflections*, C. G. Jung, p. 324).

This is why I came to the conclusion that **our greatest need in life is to be ourselves**; and the purpose of our existence is to *become* who we are. We are Soul, but not until we grow in the consciousness of our own individual self enough to realize that we are Soul will we ever satisfy the longing in our soul to be whole and complete. This is the truth above the facts of my life which my creative unconscious worked out in my novel *Cathedral of My Past Lives*, and I can only hope that I have made it palpable.

17. Pilgrimage and Penance

If I did not believe in reincarnation I would not have had seven past-life regressions; and as apprehensive as I was with each regression, I had no idea that my regressions would give me the missing pieces that would help me solve the riddle of life.

The irony was that I had already given birth to my spiritual self when Penny and I relocated to Southcentral Ontario where I met my past-life regressionist, and I no longer suffered from the longing in my soul to know who I was. **I am what I am not, and I am not what I am; I am both but neither: I am Soul.** That's how I described my spiritual birth shortly after my experience in my mother's kitchen, which speaks to the resolution of our paradoxical nature; but this only answered part of the riddle. The rest came years later when we moved to Bluewater, Georgian Bay and I had seven past-life regressions.

I learned firsthand in my regressions that we bring our karmic baggage with us from one lifetime to the next; like all of my unresolved sexual consciousness that I created in my lifetime as Salaam the Sufi in medieval Persia and further still in my lifetime as *"le salaud de Paris"* in France in the 17th Century that I had to deal with in my current lifetime, and which made my life a private hell when I accidentally awakened the "sleeping serpent" while meditating one evening in Annecy, France. And as shocked as I was to re-experience these extreme lifetimes in my regressions, they answered a lot of questions about my sexual life that puzzled me from the day I awakened to my sexuality in my early teens.

My regressions answered questions that haunted me, like the feeling that I was different and did not belong with my family; but I had no idea whatsoever that one of my regressions would provide the missing pieces to the riddle of life, and that was my regression to the Body of God where all new souls come from. "Our birth is but a sleep and a forgetting," wrote William Wordsworth in his poem *Intimations of Immortality*. "The Soul that rises with us, our life's Star, /Hath had elsewhere it's setting, /And cometh from afar: /Not in entire forgetfulness, /And not in utter nakedness, /But trailing clouds of glory do we come /From God who is our home." What the poet intimated, I experienced.

In my regression, I experienced myself as an atom of God in the Body of God, which confirmed soul's immortal nature; but I was not self-conscious. I was conscious, but I had no self-consciousness. And then, as though guided by divine providence, in the same regression I experienced the dawning of my reflective self-consciousness in my lifetime as the alpha male in a group of ten or twelve higher primates, which resolved the mystery of where the self comes from. And with each new life that I was born into, I grew in the consciousness of my reflective self; or, if you will, I grew in the new "I" of God that I gave birth to in my lifetime as a higher primate. But I had many more lives to live before I satisfied the yearning in my soul to be all that I longed to be, which brings me to my current lifetime.

When I abandoned to my creative unconscious to write *Cathedral of My Past Lives,* I was amazed if not "spooked" by how the creative spirit of my story connected the dots that formed a picture of the Divine Plan of God; and when I realized that the new "I" of God evolves in three stages through life to fulfill its destiny, life suddenly made sense to me. It was like the shades had lifted from my eyes, and I saw the meaning and purpose of life.

"Man must finish the work which nature has left incomplete," said the ancient alchemists, who had the key to the mystical transformation of our paradoxical self that nature evolves as far as possible through karma and reincarnation in the exoteric first stage of evolution; and to complete what nature cannot finish, we have to take evolution into our own hands by stepping into the mesoteric second stage of evolution, which I did when the merciful law of divine synchronicity brought Gurdjieff into my life in my second year at university.

What my creative unconscious revealed to me as I wrote *Cathedral of My Past Lives* was that nature cannot resolve the *being* and *non-being* nature of our paradoxical self through karma and reincarnation, because karma is a personal responsibility that can only be resolved through *conscious effort* and *intentional suffering,* which

Gurdjieff's teaching, my *Royal Dictum*, and the sayings of Jesus taught me how to do.

This was the *pilgrimage and penance* stage of the mesoteric stage of evolution where I gave birth to my spiritual self and initiated myself into the esoteric third stage of evolution. With indefatigable "work" on myself with *conscious effort* and *intentional suffering*, I resolved the consciousness of my *being* and *non-being* enough to shift my center of gravity (my "I") from my paradoxical self to what St. Paul called the "new creature" of my individuating Soul self; and from the moment I experienced the shift in consciousness from my outer to inner self, I knew that I was immortal and would never die. In the words of Jesus, I gave spiritual birth to myself and entered into the kingdom of God.

"Except a man be born again, he cannot see the kingdom of God," said Jesus in John's Gospel, and the only way to give birth to our spiritual self is to go through the *pilgrimage and penance* of the mesoteric second stage of evolution that transforms the consciousness of our paradoxical self; but this is so hard to do that the world has looked for shortcuts to get to the esoteric third stage that Jesus called kingdom of God but which simply means the spiritually self-realized state of our divine, Soul self.

Gurdjieff's teaching of "work" on oneself was all about the *pilgrimage and penance* stage of evolution that defines the mesoteric second stage of evolution, as was Christ's teaching of self-sacrifice; and because both teachings demand *conscious effort* and *intentional suffering* that are necessary to transform the *being* and *non-being* of our paradoxical self, I have simply called the mesoteric stage of evolution **conscious individuation.**

Despite how conscious we think we are, the exoteric first stage of evolution is all about unconscious evolution, because we are not conscious of the karmic responsibility that comes with every choice we make; but the more conscious we become of how karma works, the more we are pulled into the mesoteric stage of evolution where we learn to take evolution into our own hands to complete what nature cannot finish. And this is the irony of all the religions and teachings that seek to short-circuit the mesoteric second stage by purifying the inevitable *pilgrimage and penance* stage with the promise of instant salvation.

Gurdjieff Was Wrong But His Teaching Works

I was born into my Roman Catholic faith, and I was brought up to believe that Jesus died on the cross for my salvation because he sacrificed his life for the sins of the world; and all I had to do was confess my sins and I would be saved. I had to repent for my sins, of course; but my entrance into the kingdom of God was assured with Christ's death upon the cross, and I need not ever fear of being damned forever for my sinful life.

But as comforting as my Roman Catholic faith was, it could not satisfy the desperate longing in my soul to be my true self; and try as I may to hold onto my faith, the pull into the mesoteric second stage of evolution was so strong that I was severed from my life by a sexual experience that shocked my conscience awake and catapulted me into my quest for my true self which pulled me so deep into the *pilgrimage and penance* stage of evolution with Gurdjieff's teaching, my *Royal Dictum*, and the sayings of Jesus that I gave birth to my spiritual self in my mother's kitchen one unforgettable summer day; that's how I came to see the distinction between the religion of Christianity and Christ's secret teaching.

Christianity promises the salvation of spiritual rebirth without the *pilgrimage and penance stage* of evolution that is necessary to transform the consciousness of our paradoxical self, which is the only way we can complete what nature cannot finish; but the religion of Christianity can only make one ready for the mesoteric stage of evolution, as it did me.

Buddhism too, which short-circuits the mesoteric stage of evolution with its promise of nirvana by denying the *pilgrimage and penance* stage that is necessary to transform the *being* and *non-being* of our paradoxical self; and the New Age teaching of the Light and Sound of God that I lived for many years with its vacuous declaration that we are Soul and saved already. But these teachings only prolong the journey to our true, immortal self; and as comforting as they may seem to be, they only make one ready for the mesoteric *pilgrimage and penance* stage of evolution that completes what nature cannot finish.

As impalpable as it may be, this was my experience that gave birth to the saying that summed up my journey through the exoteric, mesoteric, and esoteric stages of evolution: **the only way out of life is**

through life. And to think that the realization of my true self was revealed to me at university with the symbolic squaring of the circle!

18. Squaring the Circle of My Life

"You needed that to get here," said St. Padre Pio in one of my spiritual healing sessions with the gifted psychic who channeled the Ascended Master for my novel *Healing with Padre Pio*; and by that he meant that the pain and anguish that I suffered for my obstinacy and stupidity was necessary to teach me the lessons that I needed to learn to grow in spirit. But I could not, and still cannot get over my humiliation for some of the decisions that I made because I did not have the wisdom to step out of my own way, like my experience with the offshoot Christian solar cult teaching that did irreparable damage to my eyesight. And yet, I am aware of the Good Saint's wisdom; and his words are a balm of healing comfort.

My story rests upon squaring the circle, my call to make the two into one, "the outer like the inner, and the male like the female neither male nor female," which in the simplest terms possible simply means resolving the paradoxical consciousness of our *being* and *non-being* nature—our lower with our higher self; and although the concept of squaring the circle implies a logical impossibility, it can be done because I experienced both the psychic manifestation of the symbolic squaring of the circle in the darkness of my bedroom in my second year at university, as well as the birth of my spiritual self in the daylight of my mother's kitchen.

I can prove neither of these experiences, which would be impossible to do in any event; but that's not the point of my story. I simply want it on record why my unconscious projected the psychic manifestation of a mandala of a yellow light squaring a circle of blue light in the darkness of my bedroom shortly after I found Gurdjieff's teaching, and how I found the secret way and did the impossible by resolving my paradoxical self; but it's not an easy story to tell because no one has ever told this story before, and like Shirley MacLaine, whom I've always admired and respected for her courage and tenacity, I feel like I'm not only out on a limb but sawing the limb off with the impalpability of my story.

I do however draw some consolation from my high school hero and literary mentor who said, "There is no use writing anything that has been written before unless you can beat it. What a writer in our time has to do is write what hasn't been written before or beat dead men at what they have done" (*By-Line: Ernest Hemingway*, pp. 217-18).

Hemingway meant literature, of course, stories on the human condition drawn from real life experience, as all of his stories and novels were; but this is the story of my life, and I don't want to couch it in fiction as I did with my spiritual healing experience that I couched in my novel *Healing with Padre Pio*. I want to tell this story because it explains the mystery of who we are, what we are, where we came from, and where we're going.

I can't begin to explain the panic I felt when the feeling possessed me that philosophy wasn't going to satisfy my need to know who I was, and I placed a lot of trust in Gurdjieff's teaching that I discovered in Ouspensky's book *In Search of the Miraculous*; but despite my instinctive attraction to Gurdjieff's teaching, it was beyond my reach and I could not find a point of entry. That's why I flung the book against the wall (or onto my desk, I can't honestly recall; but I was disgusted) and just lay on my bed and pouted before turning the light off and stretching out with my hands behind my head to wallow in self-pity.

But as I reflect on that night with 20/20 hindsight, I can't help but see that I had come to the end of the road in my quest for my true self; and, as I learned after years of living the secret way and experiencing the omniscient guiding force of life every time I came to another impasse, I'm forced to believe that my unconscious manifested the success of my quest for my true self in the symbolic squaring of the circle to lift my dejected spirits and give me the inspiration that I needed to continue on my quest for my true self—a miraculous looping of my life back upon itself to impress upon me that I would not fail, which is precisely what Jung meant in his conviction that we are all guided in life by messages from our unconscious, as I was that dark and lonely night when I felt that philosophy had failed me and I could not connect with Gurdjieff's teaching that I felt could save me.

"Dreams are the guiding words of the soul," said Jung in *The Red Book*. "Dreams pave the way for life, and they determine you without you understanding their language," which I know to be true, especially after I wrote *The Summoning of Noman* whose premise was founded upon the "guiding words" of my soul (dream messages); and as I reflect upon my lonely and desperate night when my unconscious spoke to me by manifesting a psychic symbol of a yellow light squaring a circle of blue light, I have to believe that it was a waking dream message from my unconscious telling me that I would resolve the paradox of my inner and outer self and realize my true self, despite how bleak my prospects seemed to be.

The mandala of the squaring of the circle that appeared to me at the foot of my bed was my soul's message to my mind, but I did not understand the message from my unconscious that determined me; and for many years I believed that it was a spiritual miracle that I could not share with anyone, and I drew comfort and inspiration from that symbol because on some deep level I *knew* that one day I would do the impossible and find my true self.

"Dreams pave the way for life," said Jung, and the waking dream of the mandala of my life in my bedroom at university paved my way into Gurdjieff's teaching by giving me the psychic courage to do the impossible and sacrifice the pleasures of my life with my *Royal Dictum*, which became my entry point into Gurdjieff's teaching of *conscious effort* and *intentional suffering* and the paradoxical saying of Jesus, ***"He that loveth his life shall lose it; and he that hateth his life in this world shall keep unto life eternal"*** (John 12: 25).

I don't think I'd be off the mark then to say that the manifestation of the mandala of squaring the circle was my initiation into the *pilgrimage and penance* stage of **conscious individuation** through the mesoteric stage of evolution, because shortly after this experience my creative unconscious "inspired" my *Royal Dictum* on the breakwater that memorable day as I reflected on *Ecclesiastes* and *Oedipus Rex* as I stared blankly at the Nipigon River flowing past me on its way to Lake Superior, my edict of self-denial that I vowed to live for the rest of my life that paved the way into Gurdjieff's teaching of "work on oneself" and Christ's teaching of self-sacrifice which day by day—nay, moment by bittersweet moment!— resolved the *I Am* consciousness of my *being* and *non-being* enough to make the two into one until I was ready to be reborn in my mother's kitchen that surprising summer day while she was kneading bread dough on the kitchen table.

When I reflected upon the Preacher's words as I stared at the fast-flowing waters of the Nipigon River as they swept past me to Lake Superior, the impression that they made upon me affected me viscerally; and I repeated them over and over again in my mind and then out loud for God to hear, *"All the rivers run into the sea, yet the sea is not full; unto the place from whence the rivers come, thither they return again."* And then the image of King Oedipus loomed in my mind, the boastful young man who murdered his father out of foolish pride and then married the murdered man's wife and defiled his mother's bed, whose heinous crimes one day would blight his kingdom of Thebes and the horrible price that he had to pay to save his kingdom from the blight and his own soul for his unforgivable vanity.

"Vanity of vanity, saith the Preacher, vanity of vanities; all is vanity. What profit hath a man of all his labor which he taketh under the sun?" I repeated to myself on the breakwater that day, and instantly my unconscious gave me the message of what I had to do to find my true self—I HAD TO EXILE MYSELF OUT OF MY OWN KINGDOM!

That's how I created my *Royal Dictum*, which became my entry point into Gurdjieff's teaching and my salvation; but how, exactly, did I square the circle of my life?

In her book *Striving Towards Wholeness*, Jungian analyst Barbara Hannah wrote: "In earlier days it was self-evident that every living creature was striving to complete the pattern of its existence as fully as possible. In our rational times, however, with their ever-increasing demand for specialization, this fact seems to be almost forgotten, although in the unconscious the urge toward wholeness appears to have become all the stronger for being repressed and forgotten" (*Striving Towards Wholeness*, Barbara Hannah, p. 1).

I did what I did that godforsaken night (*which I now see as the most fortunate night of my blighted life!*) that catapulted me into my quest for my true self because I could no longer repress my unconscious need for wholeness, and as repulsed and ashamed as I was for the sexual experience that severed me from my budding commercial life, it was my desperate need for wholeness that spontaneously erupted in the psychic manifestation in my bedroom that dark and lonely night when the dawning realization foreshadowed my conscious mind that philosophy was not my path to wholeness and Gurdjieff's teaching was impenetrable to me—a symbolic foretelling of my journey to my true self in the squaring of the circle.

But it would take years before I understood what my unconscious was telling me with the symbolic squaring of the circle, and I have Carl Gustav Jung to thank for that.

Quoting Goethe, one of his favorite authors and endless source of inspiration, Jung wrote in his memoir *Memories, Dreams, Reflections*: "Only gradually did I discover what the mandala really is: 'Formation, Transformation, Eternal Mind's eternal recreation.' And that is the self, the wholeness of the personality, which if all goes well is harmonious, but which cannot tolerate self-deception...It became increasingly plain to me that the mandala is the center. It is the exponent of all paths. It is the path to the center, to individuation" (*Memories, Dreams, Reflections,* C. G. Jung, pp. 195-6); and one cannot imagine the joy I felt when Jung explained in psychological terms what I had always believed to be a spiritual miracle.

My unconscious erupted my irrepressible psychic need for wholeness in the mandala of my life in the symbolic manifestation of a blue circle squared by a yellow light (blue is the colour of thought and inspiration, and yellow is the colour of spiritual light), foretelling that I would succeed in my quest for my true self; and although I did not understand the message, it eased my troubled mind and gave me the courage to seek another path, which came to me when the omniscient guiding force of life inspired me to create my *Royal Dictum*—because with my edict of self-denial I pried open what Jesus called the "straight gait" which gave me entrance into the "narrow way" of the mesoteric stage of **conscious individuation.**

The self, the wholeness of the personality, cannot tolerate self-deception, said Jung; which is precisely what my shameful experience spoke to that night when my desire for sex overpowered my sense of moral decency, because the self that did what it did that night was not me. It was me, but not me; it was my archetypal shadow. It was the false self of my soul, the *non-being* of my unconscious individuation from one lifetime to the next; and my soul could no longer suffer the oppressive karmic burden of my falseness and compelled me to find the path to wholeness in the impossible path of making the two into one which my unconscious symbolized in the squaring of the circle in my bedroom that night.

I squared the circle of my life then by "dying" to my life with my edict of self-denial, because as I denied myself the pleasures of life I "died" to my outer life and found my true, inner self; a very hard path, as Jung told Miguel Serrano, because it is next to impossible to resolve the paradoxical nature of our *being* and-*non-being*. I succeeded, as my unconscious said I would in my bedroom that night at university, only because my psychic need for wholeness was so great that I was willing to pay any price to find my true self.

Unlike the rich young merchant in Christ's parable, I paid what was asked of me to satisfy the longing in my soul and realized my eternal self in my mother's kitchen one fine day when I had resolved my paradoxical self enough to give birth to my spiritual self; but what a journey! No wonder the rich young merchant walked away—

"If thou wilt be perfect," said Jesus to him, ***"go and sell that thou hast, and give to the poor, and thou shalt have treasure in heaven; and come and follow me.*** But when the young man heard that saying, he went away sorrowful; for he had great possessions. And then Jesus said unto his disciples, ***Verily I say unto you, that a rich man shall hardly enter the kingdom of heaven. And again I say unto you, It is easier for a camel to go through the eye of a needle, than for a rich man to enter into the kingdom of heaven"*** (Matthew 19: 21-24).

Foolishly, the rich young merchant took Christ's words literally; but what was he supposed to think? He wasn't evolved enough yet to "hear" the encoded message in Christ's words to sacrifice to his outer self so he could realize his eternal self; he was still working his way through the exoteric first stage of evolution and wasn't ready yet for the mesoteric stage of **conscious individuation**. He was called but not chosen, and not until he was consumed by his unconscious need for wholeness would he hearken to the call of his soul.

Carl Jung headed the call when his soul cried out for wholeness. "The knowledge of death came to me that night…I went into the inner death and saw that outer dying is better than inner death. And I decided to die outside and live within…I turned away and sought the place of the inner life" he tells us in *The Red Book*, the chronicle of his "confrontation with the unconscious" and mythic quest for his lost soul.

"Straight is the gait, and narrow is the way, which leadeth unto life, and few there be that find it," Jesus tells us; but life is infinitely merciful, and if we don't find the secret way in this lifetime, perhaps in the next; or, as strange as it may be, in the same life should one choose to live it over again to achieve a different outcome, as I did.

19. The Story of Our Becoming

I've never kept a daily journal, as such; but I have written stories and personal essays that reflected my life at the time—like *Sparkles in the Mist* and *A Cock to Asclepius*, two unpublished books of short stories; my unpublished novel *An Atheist, An Agnostic, and Me* which reflected my life in the context of my relationship with two friends; a published novel *Tea with Grace*, and *Thoughts in Motion: Diary of a Holistic Runner,* a long and ponderous manuscript of thoughts and feelings that reflected who and what I was when I was into long distance running, plus half a dozen other unpublished works; and, in all honesty, when I re-read these works today I shudder at myself. But it is a record of what I had to work my way through to find my true self, and for that I am exceedingly thankful.

Writers don't like to rewrite their books, because they know their books reflect their time and it would be aesthetically dishonest to change them; but I'm sure many writers cringe at what they were when they wrote their books. Hemingway, for example. When he wrote *Across the River and Into the Trees* he was besotted by a young Venetian woman, which went into his novel; but the critics hated his novel and attacked him personally, and it drove him into a severe state of depression that only worsened as he got older. But *Across the River and Into the Trees* is a record of who Hemingway was at the time, and it is more revealing of the man's nature than any biography could ever be. This is why Saul Bellow's son said that if anyone wanted to know the truth about his father, all they had to do was read his novels.

And this is why I HAVE to write this story; because as personal as it may be, it transcends my life and mythologizes the archetypal hero's journey. In short, my story is the myth of my own life, my growth and individuation through the exoteric first stage of evolution and my **conscious individuation** through the mesoteric second stage of life; and because I was a seeker looking for my true self (who, happily, succeeded), the myth of my life speaks to everyone because everyone is destined to find their true self one day. That's why I believe Jung came to me in a dream one night to talk about my book

The Way of Soul; he wanted confirmation for the secret way of **conscious individuation** that leads to one's true self.

Besides, I have to get it on record that I found purpose and meaning to life that corrects Gurdjieff's misperception that man is not born with an immortal soul; which is more than I can say for many gifted writers that I have read who reflect the Gurdjieffian premise that man is not born with an immortal soul, like Vladimir Nabokov, the author of the scandalous novel *Lolita* that catapulted him into fame (or infamy, as the case may be), who wrote in his memoir *Speak Memory* that "our existence is but a brief crack of light between two eternities of darkness."

This is Nabokov's reality, and he speaks for everyone who believes that this material world is all there is to life; which is another reason why I admire and respect Carl Jung so much—because he kept an open mind to the big questions of life. He writes: "My life as I lived it had often seemed to me like a story that has no beginning and no end. I had a feeling that I was a historical fragment, an excerpt for which the preceding and succeeding text was missing. My life seemed to have been a snippet out of a long chain of events, and many questions had remained unanswered" (*Memories, Dreams, Reflections*, C.G. Jung. 291). Essentially, the same feeling as Nabokov, only more positive; but unlike Nabokov, Carl Jung devoted his life to finding an answer to these questions, and that makes his story special.

Nonetheless, there is something mystical about the creative process that engages a writer's **transcendent function** and intensifies their individuation; this is why out of all of life's pleasures, and he had many, Hemingway got the most satisfaction from writing. "Writing is something that you can never do as well as it can be done," he wrote. "It is a perpetual challenge and it is more difficult than anything else that I have ever done—so I do it. And it makes me happy when I do it well" (to Ivan Kashkin, 1935, *Selected Letters*, p.459).

But why? Why is the creative process so satisfying for the artist that they can and often do become obsessed with their art, often to the misfortune of those close to them?

Carl Jung gives us an answer, which he shares with us in his essay "Psychology and Literature" in his book *Modern Man in Search of a Soul*: "The artist is not a person endowed with free will who seeks his own ends, but one who allows art to realize its purpose through him. As a human being he may have moods and a will and personal aims, but as an artist he is 'man' in a higher sense—he is 'collective man'—one who carries and shapes the unconscious, psychic life of mankind. To perform this difficult office it is sometimes necessary for him to sacrifice happiness and everything that makes life worth living for the ordinary human being" (*Modern Man In Search of a Soul,* C. G. Jung, p. 169).

    I had such an explosion of consciousness with my seven past-life regressions that I became a man obsessed, and I HAD to write every morning before I went to work my day job as a drywall taper and housepainter; I couldn't help myself. My *daemon* possessed me, and I was up by three and four every morning to write what I felt compelled to write, and I wrote ten books in under two years—all the while working my ass off each day on my day job, because taping and sanding drywall, which was the bulk of my work, was hard work.

    Although I can't be certain, I suspect this brought on two heart attacks which led to open heart surgery; but I couldn't help myself. I had to get out what HAD to be said, but I really had no idea what HAD to be said; so I wrote, and wrote, and wrote—starting with my autobiographical novel *Cathedral of My Past Lives* to my latest memoir *The Summoning of Noman* which explores the incredible story of my parallel life through my dreams.

    But now I know why I was driven by my *daemon* to write my books, because with the explosion of consciousness that my past-life regressions released in me, I was compelled by the imperative of my *daemon* to tell the story of soul's purpose in life—which, to express it in Jungian terms, was an imperative from "the unconscious, psychic life of mankind," and I had no choice but to obey or suffer the miserable fate of the unrequited writer. But this is a mystery that needs to be explained, and the only way I can explain it is to engage my **transcendent function** and abandon to my creative unconscious…

    Hemingway had a metaphor for the magic ingredient that makes writing work, which he reveals in his memoir *A Moveable Feast* when he talks about his friend F. Scott Fitzgerald whose alcoholism ruined him as a writer; he compared Fitzgerald's natural talent to the dust on a butterflies wings, and although Hemingway doesn't spell it out in *A Moveable Feast* what this magic ingredient was that made writing work, he knew what it was because he learned this when he wrote *Green Hills of Africa*, a straight autobiographical account of his African safari that failed as a work of art because it lacked the magic ingredient that would have transformed his carefully crafted story into a work of art that would have given it flight.

So, what is the magic ingredient that Hemingway compared to the dust on a butterfly's wings if not the mystifying power of imagination? Without imagination an artist's work cannot take flight, because imagination transforms the *being* and *non-being* of the human condition and gives the work the soul it needs to take flight. This is what Norman Mailer and Martin Amis and other writers who are honest with themselves call the "spooky craft of writing," because the writer has no idea where his imagination will take their story.

Writers are called to writing, because the creative process engages their **transcendent function** and initiates them into the mesoteric stage of **conscious individuation** through the transformation of their *being* and *non-being* through writing; but very few writers (none that I know of, actually) know why they have been called. They write because they HAVE to, as they often say; but when one is ready, they will be called to the mesoteric stage of evolution to satisfy the longing in their soul to be all they are meant to be.

The creative process is the natural way to engage the **transcendent function** that transforms the consciousness of our *being* and *non-being* and makes the two into one; and when one is called to the arts, be it writing, painting, music or whatever they have evolved enough in the exoteric circle of life to step into the mesoteric circle and consciously participate in their own *becoming* through the creatively transforming process of their art.

An artist may say they do it for the money, glory, and fame; but deep down they know that their art satisfies the longing in their soul to be whole, and as egotistical as some artists may become, like my high school hero Ernest Hemingway, they participate in their own *becoming* through the creative process of their art and grow in their own identity.

But, sadly, art is not enough to satisfy the longing in one's soul for wholeness; and unless the artist finds another path to initiate them deeper into the mesoteric stage of evolution, they will suffer the artist's anguish of being unrequited, which can drive an artist to despair and possibly suicide, as it did Ernest Hemingway. "Look," said Hemingway to his friend Hotch, "it doesn't matter that I don't write for a day or a year or ten years as long as the knowledge that I *can* write is solid inside me. But a day without that knowledge, or not being sure of it, is eternity" (*Papa Hemingway*, A. E. Hotchner, p. 298).

As therapy for his "black-ass" depression, Hemingway had electroshock treatment at the Mayo Clinic in Rochester, which ruined his memory upon which he relied to write his stories (his fourth wife Mary said that his mind was like a tape recorder); and unable to engage his **transcendent function** through writing, Hemingway could no longer nourish his soul through the creative transformation of his *being* and *non-being,* or making the two into one through his stories; that's what drove him to take his own life with his favorite shotgun.

"Hotch, I can't finish the book. I *can't.* I've been at this goddamn worktable all day, standing here all day, all I've got to get is this one thing, maybe only a sentence, maybe more, I don't know, and I can't get it. Not any of it. You understand, I *can't,*" he said to his friend, and sometime later added with characteristic Hemingway defiance, "Hotch, if I can't exist on my own terms, then existence is impossible. Do you understand? That's how I've lived, and that is how I must live—or not live" (*Papa Hemingway*, p. 285 and 297).

And herein lies the deep mystery of **conscious individuation,** which Jesus tried to reveal to the rich young merchant who wanted to know how to gain eternal life; the secret that revealed itself to me as I "worked" on myself with Gurdjieff's teaching, my *Royal Dictum*, and the sayings of Jesus—the secret of self-sacrifice.

But before I reveal the deep secret of **conscious individuation**, let me share what I have learned about the mystical power of story; and I use the word "mystical" deliberately, because there is a mystical quality to every story that affects us without us understanding why. As the saying goes, everyone loves a good love story; and the reason we love a good love story is because there is something inherently satisfying about it. But as I have come to realize, this can be said of all stories; in some mysterious way they nourish the longing in our soul to know who we are, what we are, where we come from, and where we are going.

Unfortunately, as the talented writer Katherine Mansfield came to realize, literature is not enough to satisfy the longing in our soul for wholeness, which is why we never tire of stories—vainly hoping that the next story we read or watch on TV or movie theater will satisfy our need to know; but what is it that story gives us that only whets our appetite for more?

I gave this question to my creative unconscious when I wrote my book *The Pearl of Great Price*, which was my exploration of Christ's most precious parable; and the answer that my **transcendent function** provided for me came to me in Chapter 18 which, coincidentally, is called "The Dust on a Butterfly's Wings." If I may, let me quote the entire passage because it speaks to the heart of the mystery of story and the individuation process:

"Stories bear the truth of the human condition, and the human condition is the story of our becoming; but not until we solve the riddle of our becoming will literature resolve the issue of the human condition. This makes literature endlessly fascinating, because every writer speaks to their place in the enantiodromiac process of man's *becoming*, which Jung called 'individuation,' and in their stories they stake out the geography of man's soul, whether it be the happy country of one's *being*, the unhappy country of one's *non-being*, or that miserable place of being stuck between two countries—the no-man's land of one's soul."

Truth. This is what stories give us; the truth born of the *becoming* process of the human condition. This is what we long for—the truth of life. And every story that we ingest nourishes our need to know the truth of life; that's why we never tire of stories. And that's why writers say that they write to get to the truth of life. Nay, they are compelled by the imperative of their calling to tell the truth of life. As Joyce Carole Oates, one of the most prolific writers in America today, said in her book *The Faith of a Writer*: "The writer's first thought is, *I have to tell*. And the writer's second thought is, *how do I tell it?*"

This is the lure and power of story. But, sad to say, literature—art, for that matter—is not enough to satisfy the longing in our soul to know who we are, what we are, where we came from, and where we're going—which in effect is our longing for wholeness; and the only way to satisfy our longing is by taking evolution into our own hands in the mesoteric circle of evolution and master the art of making the two into one—as I learned to do with Gurdjieff's teaching, my *Royal Dictum*, and the sayings of Jesus. Which brings me to the deep secret of **conscious individuation** that art opens us up to.

The artist, be he a writer, painter, musician or whatever, engages their **transcendent function** and transforms the consciousness of their *being* and *non-being* through the creative dialectic of their art; this is why a writer HAS to write and the artist HAS to paint and the musician HAS to play music—because the artist satisfies the longing in their soul for wholeness with their art. Their art is their *becoming,* their path to individuation; but, because art cannot satisfy our longing for wholeness, we have to find a path that is more satisfying—as Katherine Mansfield did with Gurdjieff's teaching and Jerry Wennstrom did by initiating himself deep into the mystery of **conscious individuation** through self-sacrifice.

What, then, is this deep mystery of the mesoteric circle of evolution that satisfies the longing in our soul for wholeness? And if I may, just to play the devil's advocate, how can one be certain that this is nothing more than philosophical speculation?

The sad truth is that one can never be certain until one experiences the mystery, which I did when I gave birth to my spiritual self in my mother's kitchen that day; because from that moment on I no longer longed to be who I was because I had *become* myself. In one totally unexpected moment I coincided with myself and *became* myself; or, in Christ's words, the two became one in me, and I no longer longed to *be*. And I articulated my experience in the following words: **I am what I am not, and I am not what I am; I am both, but neither. I am Soul**. This was and is my state of consciousness today; so I know from personal experience that the deep secret of **conscious individuation** is self-sacrifice.

This sounds terrifying, but the deep secret of self-sacrifice simply means the mystical art of transforming the consciousness of our paradoxical self and making the two into one; and by one I simply mean an unselfish self—a self that is both *being* and *non-being* and neither; a self that transcends both our *being* and *non-being*, which is our individuated Soul self. And art, for all of its truth above the facts of life, simply cannot satisfy our longing for wholeness; the most that art can do is bring us to the "strait gait" which opens onto the "narrow way" of self-sacrifice—as it did with the contemporary artist Jerry Wennstrom.

Writers like Nabokov then get stuck in the *non-being* state of their *becoming*, that place in the geography of their soul where they cannot fathom their existence before the birth and after the death of their "mortal coil," whereas writers like Wordsworth take us right to heaven's gate and give us a glimpse of the glory that is ours to achieve—which is what I came back to do in my current parallel life; and as strange as it may be, it's all true.

20. The Transcendent Self

This is the age of the consumer, and practically anything we want can be ours for the taking (with enough money we can have practically anything); this is why the concept of self-sacrifice today is so repelling. Our every desire can be satisfied in our consumer market, and the good life has become the ideal to strive for; but for all of the pleasure that the good life may give us (travel, golf, shopping), it will not satisfy our longing to be whole. This is why we often hear people say, "I've got everything, but I'm not happy."

That was the rich young merchant's dilemma in Christ's parable. He was a good person who had obeyed the commandments of God from his youth, and he had enough wealth to make him happy, but still he longed for eternal life; that's why he asked Jesus what he had to do to have eternal life. He heard the call to wholeness, and Jesus gave him a solution to his dilemma; but the rich young merchant wasn't ready to heed the call.

This is a hard parable. ***"It is easier for a camel to go through the eye of a needle, than for a rich man to enter into the kingdom of God,"*** said Jesus, and every wealthy Christian has quaked in their shoes since Jesus uttered those words; but like the rich young merchant, the wealthy Christian (and non-Christian) need not worry about giving their wealth away to enter into the kingdom of eternal life, because that's not what Jesus meant by his saying.

The key to understanding Christ's message of salvation lies in the esoteric knowledge of man's dual nature, his *being* and *non-being*, or paradoxical self, if you will; and all of Christ's teaching has to do with what Jesus referred to as "making the two into one."

Not only is the parable of the rich young merchant one of Christ's sternest messages, it is also one of his deepest; and it took me a long time to decode it. I had already given birth to my spiritual self when I broke the code of this parable, and when I did I could hardly believe how simple his message was—as are all of Christ's sayings and parables when one finds the key that unlocks their mystery; and the key is the **transcendent self**.

The **transcendent self** is our divine nature, the individuating consciousness of our immortal soul that is born from life to life to grow in what it is meant to be through its karmic destiny, just as Jung intuited in an interview for the BBC: "As each plant grows from a seed and becomes in the end an oak tree, so man becomes what he is meant to be. He ought to get there, but most get stuck." That's why the rich young merchant went to Jesus; he was stuck.

This is the deep mystery of the Christ's parable of the rich young merchant. For the record, let me quote the parable first and then decode the message, which speaks to the mesoteric stage of **conscious individuation** through self-sacrifice:—

"And, behold, one came and said unto him, Good Master, what good thing shall I do, that I may have eternal life?

"And he said unto him, *Why callest me thou good? There is none good but one, that is, God; but if thou wilt enter into life, keep the commandments.*

"He said unto him, which? Jesus said, *Thou shalt do no murder, Thou shalt not commit adultery, Thou shalt not steal, Thou shalt not bear false witness, Honor thy father and thy mother: and, Thou shalt love thy neighbor as thyself.*

"The young man said unto him, All these things have I kept from my youth up: what lack I yet?

"Jesus said unto him, *If thou wilt be perfect, go and sell that thou hast, and give it to the poor, and thou shalt have treasure in heaven; and come and follow me.*

"But when the young man heard that saying, he went away sorrowful: for he had great possessions.

"Then Jesus said unto his disciples, *Verily I say unto you, That a rich man shall hardly enter the kingdom of heaven.*

"And again I say unto you, It is easier for a camel to go through the eye of a needle, than for a rich man to enter into the kingdom of God" (Matthew: 19: 16-24).

For the longest time I puzzled over this parable, because I could not fathom what Jesus meant by implying that one had to do more than keep the commandments to gain eternal life, which the rich young merchant had done from his youth; but when I connected the dots and realized what Jesus meant when he told him what else he had to do for eternal life, his message became crystal clear to me because the key that unlocks the door to the kingdom of eternal life is self-sacrifice—meaning, the wealthy consciousness of our *non-being*.

Seeing that the rich young merchant had obeyed the commandments of God from his youth, Jesus saw him to be a good man; but being good was not enough to enter into the kingdom of heaven. He had to be perfect, and to be perfect he had to sacrifice what was imperfect—which was the false self of his *non-being*. But the rich young merchant was stuck in the exoteric circle of life, and he took Christ's message literally and walked away because he could not step into the mesoteric stage of evolution and perfect his consciousness by sacrificing the imperfect consciousness of his false self—his wealthy ego self, if you will.

And that's exactly what I had done with my *Royal Dictum* and Gurdjieff's teaching of *conscious effort* and *intentional suffering*; as I sacrificed my outer life of pleasure and desire I grew in the consciousness of my neither/nor **transcendent self** until I had grown enough to shift my center of gravity (my "I") from my outer self to my inner self, and I experienced the birth of my eternal self in my mother's kitchen that unforgettable day.

Our **transcendent self** is our divine nature, our soul self that is individuated through the *enantiodromiac* dynamic of the *being* and *non-being* of our outer self, which we do naturally in the exoteric circle of life through karma and reincarnation; and not until we have grown enough in our soul self will we be called to the mesoteric circle of evolution where we can transform the consciousness of our *being* and *non-being* and make the two into one and satisfy the longing in our soul to be what we are meant to be.

It was a hard truth, but once I broke the code of Christ's parable of the rich young merchant I finally resolved a mystery that haunted me for years. In all my years of living the life of the secret way, I was never able to resolve the mystery of why good people suffered the dread of spiritual doubt; like Mother Teresa, for example. Why?

Why would a woman who devoted her life to caring for the poor suffer spiritual doubt? She obeyed the commandments of God.

She was a good person. Why would she suffer such dark nights of the soul, as has been revealed since her death?

The only answer that I can offer comes from personal experience, which speaks to the mystery of our **transcendent self**; and as presumptuous as it may be, it has to do with the unresolved nature of our *being* and *non-being*—or paradoxical self, if you will. And not until we resolve our paradoxical self enough to shift our center of gravity from our outer to inner self will we stop having spiritual doubt—because spiritual doubt is born of the *enantiodromiac* life-and-death dynamic of our *becoming,* and not our **transcendent self**.

In all honesty (and I don't expect anyone to believe me), when I shifted my center of gravity from my outer to inner self in my mother's kitchen that day, I never again suffered spiritual doubt; I knew that I was immortal, and all spiritual doubt ceased to be. The longing in my soul left me, and I never again yearned to be myself. In one glorious moment I slid out of my outer self and slipped into my inner self, and my life changed forever.

It's a difficult concept to apprehend, but the "I" of our outer self is the same "I" of our inner self; and purifying the consciousness of our outer self is what Jesus meant by perfecting ourselves. This is what Socrates also meant when he said in the *Phaedo*, "And what is purification but the separation of the soul from the body, as I was saying before; the habit of soul gathering and collecting herself into herself." And as we gather and collect the "I" of our outer self into the "I" of our inner self, we make the two into one and realize our **transcendent self**. That's the gist of Christ's parable of the rich young merchant and the secret teaching of salvation that Jesus encoded in his sayings and parables, which became the premise of Gurdjieff's teaching of "work" oneself through *conscious effort* and *intentional suffering*; and despite the fact that Gurdjieff did not believe that man is born with an immortal soul, his teaching works all the same because it transforms the consciousness of our *being* and *non-being* egoic self into the consciousness of our **transcendent self.**

21. The Essential Gurdjieff

I read Gurdjieff's behemothian opus *All and Everything: Beelzebub's Tales to his Grandson* once, and that was enough for me; and although I could have made this book my life's study, as many students of Gurdjieff's teaching have, I had to ask myself: why bother?

I grasped the essence of Gurdjieff's teaching as I initiated myself into the secret way of life with *conscious effort* and *intentional suffering*, and making a detailed study of *All and Everything* seemed redundant and a colossal waste of time; so I put it away and got on with the business of living my destined purpose, which was to become a writer.

A writer has their own voice, which does not come easily. Some writers are born with it, and others have to acquire it; I had to acquire mine. But to acquire my own voice, I had to find myself first; that's why I became a seeker before I became a writer.

I said that I became a seeker in high school with Somerset Maugham's novel *The Razor's Edge*, but that only fanned the flame of the fire in me; and when I had the sexual experience in my early twenties that shocked my conscience awake, I divested my business interests and fled to France to begin my quest for my true self; and after living a year in the Alpine city of Annecy in the *Haute Savoie* region of France, I returned to Canada to study philosophy at Lakehead University, an hour's drive from my hometown of Nipigon where I started my own painting business after dropping out of university in my third year.

I found Gurdjieff at university, which I now believe was my reason for going to university in the first place despite whatever reasons I may have given—like studying the "mother of all disciplines" to find the answer to the burning question of my life, *who am I?* But for whatever reason I went, the result was that Gurdjieff introduced me to a teaching that would initiate me into the secret way of life, which led me to my true self; and for that I will always be grateful to Gurdjieff and his Fourth Way teaching.

Gurdjieff Was Wrong But His Teaching Works

But once I found my true self—which in Gurdjieffian terms meant that I had "created" my own immortal soul—I no longer needed Gurdjieff's teaching; and so I moved on to another path, a New Age teaching of the Light and Sound of God; an ancient spiritual path neatly woven together out of various Eastern teachings by a very clever writer, but which took me more than thirty years to realize was authentic at its core but fraudulent in its premise with its unbroken line of "imagined" Spiritual Masters going far back into antiquity but with no empirical evidence to support it, and a God-realized Spiritual Leader who assumed the title of Inner Master as well as Dream Master and purported to guide us from within but which I was never comfortable with because I *knew* that my Inner Self and I were one.

I dropped this teaching upon completing my book *The Pearl of Great Price* in the spring of 2015, because I had acquired my own voice and realized that writing was my life's path; and, if I'm to believe a precognitive dream that I had a few years ago, will also be my path in my next incarnation because I will be born with a remarkable talent for writing; but what does this have to do with Gurdjieff's teaching and squaring the circle?

Everything, because the essential purpose of Gurdjieff's teaching of "work on oneself" was to do the impossible and "create" my own soul—regardless how deep he had "buried the bone," as Gurdjieff liked to do. And that's what's always bothered me about Gurdjieff's writing, because his literary conceit was to bury every little nugget of precious knowledge so the seeker had to dig for it; only then would one appreciate his teaching.

Undoubtedly, Gurdjieff came by his literary conceit honestly since he had to dig long and hard and deep for the precious knowledge that he found in his efforts to answer the haunting question of his life. From an early age, Gurdjieff had "an unquenchable aspiration to understand the precise meaning of the life process of all the outward forms of breathing creatures on Earth, and especially the aim of human life."

Along with a group of like-minded associates calling themselves "Seekers of Truth," Gurdjieff set out travelling throughout Central Asia and the Far East in search of ancient knowledge, and after twenty years of digging he collected a body of esoteric knowledge that he collated into his Fourth Way teaching which he brought to the western world. **"I have very good leather to sell for those who want to make themselves shoes,"** said Gurdjieff; and the price for his "very good leather" was effort—long, hard, indefatigable conscious effort.

Gurdjieff believed that to gain any understanding at all, we are forced to dig. When we dig, we work; we persevere. And finally, we find! And then every hard-won nugget of precious knowledge becomes our own, an integral part of our understanding. That's why Gurdjieff wrote the way he did; but I hated it with a passion.

I couldn't explain why, but I always felt there was something wrong with this method of transmitting the ancient knowledge; and once I found the key in my *Royal Dictum* that unlocked the "strait gate" of the "narrow way," I stopped digging in Gurdjieff's books to find those precious little nuggets of knowledge that he had hidden in his writing.

I leaned towards the school of thought that when one finds the secret way he is obligated to let his light shine for everyone to see and not hide it under a bushel or conceal it in writing so obfuscating that one can drive oneself silly digging. Not that all of those nuggets of truth hidden in his writing—*All and Everything, Meetings with Remarkable Men*, and *Life Is Real Only Then, When I Am*—weren't precious and worth looking for; but because the essence of Gurdjieff's teaching was the key to "creating" one's own soul all of that esoteric knowledge about man and the cosmos that he had buried in his impenetrable body of writing was unnecessary to my purpose of realizing my true self.

The irony of course is that one does not have to "create" their own soul because we are all born with an immortal soul, and the purpose of our life is to grow in the consciousness of our own immortal nature and become who we are meant to be; but Gurdjieff's teaching precipitated the process of **conscious individuation**, which is why I love and respect him for his Fourth Way teaching despite his premise that man is not born with an immortal soul.

So, what exactly is the essence of Gurdjieff's teaching that makes of the precious nuggets of knowledge buried in his body of writing moot to one's purpose of "creating" one's own soul? What is the key to Gurdjieff's teaching of the Fourth Way?

Gurdjieff Was Wrong But His Teaching Works

Because Gurdjieff believed that man is not born with an immortal soul, his teaching takes into account the whole nature of man—his physical, emotional, and mental nature; and only by understanding how each aspect of our nature functions can we "work" on ourselves and create our own immortal soul. This is what makes Gurdjieff's teaching so complex and intimidating; but I saw something in his teaching that I couldn't put my finger on, and I persisted until his teaching drove me to create my *Royal Dictum* which unlocked the mystical secret of Gurdjieff's teaching of "work on oneself."

I have deliberately put quotation marks around this phrase, because this kind of work is special insomuch that it transforms the consciousness of our *being* and *non-being* and makes the two into one, as Jesus taught with his sayings and parables. **So the key to understanding Gurdjieff's teaching of "work on oneself" is the knowledge that we can "create" our own immortal soul out of the consciousness of our *being* and *non-being*;** and it does not matter if he did not believe that we are already born with an immortal soul.

Gurdjieff's teaching works all the same, because it initiates one into the mesoteric stage of **conscious individuation**; and once one learns the secret of how to nourish his inner self with *conscious effort* and *intentional suffering* (plus his other techniques of *self-remembering* and *non-identifying*), one will grow in the consciousness of his inner self and realize their immortal self one day, as I experienced. That's how I know that Gurdjieff's teaching works, despite his premise that we are not born with an immortal soul.

Naturally, I came to the realization that Gurdjieff's premise was wrong long after I gave birth to my spiritual self in my mother's kitchen that day, because I had to do a lot more growing before I came to see that Soul is who we are, and *realizing* that we are Soul is what the purpose of the Divine Plan of God is all about; that's why I was called to the Way of the Eternal, because this New Age teaching that was drawn from ancient sources introduced me to spiritual concepts that helped me to grow in my understanding of life's purpose—despite its fraudulent premise and fictional mythological history. As St. Padre Pio told me in one of my spiritual healing sessions, "you needed that to get here." And where is "here"?

"Here" is my comfortable understanding that no one path to God is more relevant than another, however true or false it may be, because life is an individual journey and we have forever to realize our true self; which in one fell stroke eliminates all of the insufferable anxiety of our mortality.

"Here" is the happy realization that it doesn't matter if we don't succeed today, because we have forever to try again—as I did by returning to live my same life over again to achieve what I failed to achieve in my first lifetime as Orest Stocco.

"Here" is a very strange place to be, because no one will understand where "here" is until they initiate themselves into the mystery of who they are; and for this, once again, I have to thank Gurdjieff who introduced me to the secret way that led me to my true self.

But I wouldn't wish Gurdjieff's teaching upon anyone, because it is a very difficult teaching to live by if one accepts his premise that we are not born with an immortal soul; that's why I love what St. Padre Pio said about the secret way: **"Learn to love what you do, and do what you love; that is the way into the Heart of God and happiness."**

"Here" is being my own path through life...

22. A Place Called Sanctuary

"I hate it when you go to sanctuary. I just hate it," Penny would say to me whenever I withdrew to my safe place from the world of hurt and misunderstanding; a place, I liked to say, so remote that not even God could reach me. That's what Gurdjieff's technique of *non-identifying* did for me, among other things—like creating an energy field around me so powerful that it kept the summer mosquitoes from biting me, if one can believe that.

I realized this while watching a ball game at the Nipigon Arena one evening. There was a young lady watching the game also with whom I had made love to once on my waterbed; but because of the "flip" I *non-identified* with her to keep from desiring her.

The "flip" was a technique that I came up with to let go and let God when I felt I had come to another dead end on my path to wholeness. What inspired my "flip" technique was the question: *how can I be certain that the choices I make are the right choices?*

I was deep into my Gurdjieffian path of "work on oneself," but I had no one to share my thoughts with because I hadn't come across anyone else who had even heard of Gurdjieff, let alone read him, not even at university; so I had to puzzle my way through his Fourth Way teaching as I forged my own way through life. But I came to a dead end, very much like I did when I could make no headway into Gurdjieff's teaching and created my *Royal Dictum.*

My *Royal Dictum* initiated me into the secret teaching of "work on oneself," which Gurdjieff had appropriated for his Fourth Way teaching but which in reality was the basic spiritual practice of the Sufi teaching that I gravitated to as I "worked" on myself in that special way that transformed the consciousness of my lower self, that special kind of gnostic wisdom that I began to see in all sayings and aphorisms; but my personal path had brought me as far as it could and I came to a dead end and I did not know what to do.

"Do I go right, do I go left; which way am I to go? Do I do this, do I do that; what am I to do?" I didn't know. Today I know it doesn't matter what choice we make because there is no such thing as right or wrong choices in life, only choices that will take us where we will get to eventually because we are all pre-destined to realize our true self; but at that time in my life it was vital for me to know that the choice I made was the right choice, but how could I be certain? I was desperate. Not quite as desperate as when I created my *Royal Dictum*, but desperate enough to once again do something drastic; and so my creative unconscious came up with the brilliant idea to let go and let God decide for me with the flip of a coin!

Try to imagine the desperation I must have felt to abandon my life to the flip of a coin, the audacity to believe that God would decide for me; but I did. I put my faith in the flip of a coin, letting God make up my mind for me. Of course, I couldn't be certain it was God that would decide for me; but I had to believe that God would choose for me, because I couldn't abandon my life to random chance; could I? That would be foolhardy.

Had I shared this technique with anyone, they would have thought that it was not only reckless, but crazy; but for six months I flipped my coin to make my mind up for me. But only the big decisions. I was capable of making up my own mind with the small decisions; and by big decisions I mean a decision like asking the young lady that I had made love with on my waterbed one evening after the bar closed if she would go out with me.

I flipped my coin and said, "Heads I ask her out, tails I don't." The coin landed tails, and I never pursued my romantic interest. That's why at the ball game at the Nipigon Arena that evening I practiced the Gurdjieffian technique of *non-identifying* with her so that I could go to sanctuary where my desire for her would not affect me.

Sanctuary was a very special place that I created with the technique of *non-identifying* with the objects of my desire or interest—be they physical, emotional, or intellectual. Sanctuary was a state of neither/nor consciousness; a place of total indifference, which was why Penny just hated it when I went to sanctuary.

It didn't matter how much she loved me or I loved her, when I went to sanctuary even love could not reach me. I didn't know it at the time, but this was the state of consciousness that I shifted my center of gravity (my "I") to when I gave birth to my spiritual self in my mother's kitchen that summer day; that's why I could say, **I am**

what I am not, and I am not what I am; I am both but neither. I am Soul. Sanctuary was where I made the two into one (my *being* and *non-being*) and realized my true self.

But this was a long, hard, and difficult process because **conscious individuation** takes enormous effort. That's why I concluded that to *be* our true self we have to *become* our true self, which awakened me to the fallacy of instant salvation that Christianity promises.

Going to sanctuary was another *pilgrimage and penance* stage of my *becoming*, and it took enormous effort to *non-identify* with the objects of my desire, especially romantic interests; that's how I exhausted myself and decided to let go and let God decide for me with the flip of a coin. It gave me a rest from the enormous responsibility of choosing for myself. But somewhere in the fourth month I began to notice a strange pattern whenever I let go and let God decide for me: *I noticed that my coin always agreed with my gut feeling!*

Whenever I had a tough decision to make and my gut told me what I should DO, my coin agreed with my gut feeling; and whenever my gut told me NOT to do something, my coin also agreed with my gut feeling. This pattern was so consistent—every single time I flipped the coin in fact, which defied the laws of chance!—that I finally concluded that my gut feeling was my Higher Self advising me; and that's when I made the connection and realized that **my will was one with God's will whenever I trusted my own gut feeling!**

As I reflected upon this outrageous commitment to let my coin decide what I should do, I realized that I was honing my powers of intuition; and the more I let go and let God decide for me, the more I learned to trust my own judgment—but only if I was true to the flip. I could not let my coin decide for me and then do the opposite. That would have defeated the purpose of the whole experiment and negate the very premise of my exercise.

Total trust in the flip led to total trust in myself, and I abandoned the flip technique and got on with my life as though nothing had happened; and my family, friends, and customers were none the wiser. *But what a journey it was letting a coin decide for me!*

I tried for years to write a story about my experience with the flip of a coin, but I could never get my story started; and I had to wait a few more years for the story to gestate in my unconscious.

Finally the story sprouted, but only because I gave my experience to another character in my story, a man I knew very well who became the model for my protagonist Jordan Hansen to whom I gave the technique of the flip to make up his mind for him; but the working title for my novel "The Flip" changed to what my published novel is today, *The Golden Seed*.

I got the surprise of my life with what my creative unconscious did with this technique of letting the coin decide Jordan's mind; and when I finished writing this novel I confirmed what I always felt about the creative process, which gave me a whole new respect for creative writers because they are the bearers of the truth of life.

A novel gives birth to its own truth, and *The Golden Seed* gave birth to the truth that **our will and God's will are one and the same, but only when our will coincides with God's will.** When our will chooses a path that strays from our pre-destined purpose of realizing our divine nature, then we suffer the karmic fate of disconnecting with our inner self; and not until we align our will with God's will of our pre-destined purpose will we connect with our inner self and be happy with our life.

Jordan made a stupid and selfish decision when he abandoned his wife and family for the woman who seduced him when he was at his most vulnerable, and my story had to do with how he could redeem himself from his terrible decision; that's why I introduced the flip into his life. But in all honesty, I had no idea how my creative unconscious was going to use the flip to redeem Jordan from his bad decision; but I trusted the creative process, and my story took flight when I let my imagination work it out. And that's the "spooky craft of writing" that never ceases to amaze creative writers.

But I would never have had the courage to try such a bold experiment had I not mastered Gurdjieff's technique of *non-identifying*, because with this technique I created a state of consciousness that transcended my life and gave me the power to do.

"The highest that man can attain is to be able to do," said Gurdjieff, summarizing the goal of his teaching; and the more I grew in that place called sanctuary, the more I was able to do. That's why I risked my promising future and divested myself of my business interests and fled to France to find my true self; and why I dared to risk my university degree by following my gut feeling and going out into the world to find my own way; and why I started my own painting business by slapping two magnetic signs on my 1967 Camaro with little to no experience; and how I built my mortgage-free triplex with only nineteen dollars in my bank account and a minimum of carpentry skills; and why I wrote a novel that so shocked my hometown that Penny and I had to relocate to Georgian Bay for peace of mind; and how I got to solve the riddle of life by trusting my gut feeling and having seven past-life regressions that gave me the missing pieces to the puzzle, and then having a spiritual healing with St. Padre Pio that slew the vanity of my spiritual conceit that was fed by the unconscious *shadow* personality of my spiritual community which vaunted to be on "the most direct path to God," and which became the basis of my novel *Healing with Padre Pio*; I was able to do what I did, because I had become who I was—which confirmed what Gurdjieff said that to be able to do one must first *be;* and this is what inspired my favourite poem that puts the whole Gurdjieffian philosophy of life into poetic perspective—

I Am
I felt ashamed of life when I saw her frail body
fighting for its life in the Emergency Room,
emaciated, and heaving like a bellows for air;
I saw no dignity in the physical struggle
to stay alive, no grace, no love, no honor,
just a bodily organism in the throes of death.
I walked home alone from the hospital,
the lonely moon as big as the Eye of God
and the stars sparkling like lost souls in heaven,
and I thought of life and death and everything
in between, and in my heart I smiled for all
of my efforts, struggles, and humiliations to find
my true self, because as I spied death steal my lover's
mother's life I knew, I simply knew, that I am,
and life is merely something that I do.

23. Blazing My Own Trail

I regret not having a personal mentor, because it costs to blaze one's own trail. It costs so much that if one makes it to his senior years without having compromised himself to "Old Whore Life," he will have plenty of scars to show for it; and I have scars that I'm still too embarrassed to write about, like my experience with that offshoot Christian solar cult teaching that did irreparable damage to my eyesight, my sexual experience that brutally shocked my conscience awake, and my relationship with my family.

Aside from a burning curiosity to know about my past lives, I wanted to find out why I did not fit in with my family; and my first past-life regression brought me back to my immediate past lifetime in London, England where every member of my family except my father were members of the privileged British aristocracy; my father was a commoner, which was why my mother always treated my father like he was never good enough for her. I was destined to find my own way in life, which I began to do when I fled the aristocracy and sailed to the Americas to become a fur trapper.

The trail that I began to blaze in my immediate past lifetime brought me to a gifted medium in my current life who channeled St. Padre Pio, whom I was destined to meet because according to him we had planned our meeting on the Other Side; and he gave me a whole new perspective on reincarnation when he told me that I had lived my same life over again on three separate occasions, and my current lifetime was such an occasion. Apparently, I had not achieved what I had been born to achieve in my first lifetime as Orest Stocco; but in my second lifetime as Orest Stocco I achieved my goal of transcending myself, which St. Padre Pio confirmed in my tenth and final spiritual healing session with the gifted medium.

This is the subject of my memoir *The Summoning of Noman*, which is the story of how I was summoned to God for a reckoning and was found wanting; and the goal of my current lifetime was to find my lost soul which belonged to God. This is why I had to blaze my own trail in life, because no one knew where I had lost my soul but me.

According to Gurdjieff, man is not born with an immortal soul; only with the potential to create one, and his teaching accelerated one's potential for immortality. That's why his teaching attracted people who felt the oppressive burden of their own *non-being,* like it attracted me to Ouspensky's book *In Search of the Miraculous* which is still today considered to be the best exposition of Gurdjieff's teaching; but why Gurdjieff? Why not another teaching? What was it about Gurdjieff's teaching that spoke to me?

Was it because Gurdjieff had blazed his own trail? Was that what brought me to his teaching, because it would teach me how to blaze my own trail?

I've given this a lot of thought over the years, and the conclusion that was forced upon me from all the literature that I read and personal experiences with the omniscient guiding force of life—which manifests in various ways to show us the way we are meant to go; signs, symbols, dreams, and meaningful coincidences—is that we do not choose the path we take in life; instead, **OUR PATH CHOOSES US**.

Take the way I found Gurdjieff's teaching, for example. My philosophy studies were coming to an end, because philosophy could not satisfy my *daemonic* need to know who I was; and the omniscient guiding force of life initiated my introduction to Gurdjieff's teaching by having a fellow student bring me a book from his favorite bookstore in Toronto when he went home for the Christmas break, a book that I had no knowledge of; that's how P. D. Ouspensky's book *In Search of the Miraculous* came into my possession.

This experience (among others that blessed me with similar good fortune) convinced me that when a person is ready for the next stage of their journey through life, a path will present itself by way of a book, a person, a new career opportunity or whatever; and upon reflection I can see that Gurdjieff's teaching chose me because that's the path I needed to continue my quest for my true self. But why? Why did I need Gurdjieff's teaching?

The logic is simple, but devastating. Gurdjieff's teaching is founded upon the premise that man must "create" his own soul through his own *conscious effort* and *intentional suffering*. No one can "create" their immortal soul for them; and Gurdjieff's teaching gave me the secret knowledge of how to precipitate my own spiritual growth. Gurdjieff and a group of fellow Seekers of Truth scoured the world of ancient cultures for this hidden knowledge, and when he came to the west he initiated an esoteric school to pass on this knowledge to wake man up from "the hypnotic sleep of life," a teaching that he called the Fourth Way which combined the way of the body (physical effort, like special dancing which Gurdjieff taught); the way of emotions (like music, which Gurdjieff also used for esoteric purposes); and by way of the mind (special mental exercises)—all to speed up the process of "creating" one's own soul. But, as I said, I did not know of anyone else who had even heard of Gurdjieff and his teaching, and I had to be extremely innovative in my efforts to transform the consciousness of my *being* and *non-being* and transcend myself.

In effect, life became both my school and my teacher; and my lessons were hard and my teacher cruel. That's how I came to call life an "Old Whore." My exact words, which I recorded somewhere in one of my notebooks, were: *"Life is like an old whore who squats obscenely upon my shoulders and screws me of my virtue every chance she gets!"*

Many years later, a lot more mellow but still subject to the unpredictable whims of "Old Whore Life," I wrote a book of spiritual musings called *Old Whore Life, Exploring the Shadow Side of Karma*, because I had finally come to see that the "Old Whore" who screws us of our virtue is our own karmic obtuseness; and then one day I finally gave up the ghost of "Old Whore Life" and accepted full karmic responsibility for my life—which, to add insult to injury, inspired my next book of spiritual musings, *Stupidity Is Not A Gift of God*; and I have Gurdjieff to thank for that, because his teaching compelled me to take risks in my life that garnered me a lot of wisdom but cost me more than I care to say, like studying an offshoot Christian solar cult teaching that did irreparable damage to my eyesight.

I hope one day to write the story of my involvement with this offshoot Christian solar cult teaching that I found advertised in *Psychology Today* magazine and which I studied by correspondence for three years and which attracted me because of the Gurdjieffian secret "way of the sly man" that taught me how to cheat the devil of his illicit share of life energy; but for now, suffice to say that this teaching brought me face to face with a Shadow Master when I flew to Reno, Nevada for a weekend study session with the spiritual leader of this cult teaching, a man whose personal energy was so false that I dropped the teaching the day after shaking his hand but nonetheless suffered the consequence of the solar techniques that burnt three pin holes in the retina of my eyes, and I simply have to write this story one day.

It's easy to judge a person after the fact, as I judged myself for my unbelievable naiveté—stupidity would be more appropriate, which was how my ophthalmologist in Thunder Bay reacted when he learned how I had burnt three holes in my eyes and refused to treat me and I had to get my brother in Waterloo to set up an appointment for me in the Eye Clinic in Waterloo; but unless one has experienced what it means to be caught in the grip of one's own *daemon*, one will never understand what drives a seeker, and I was driven to extremes by my need to nourish the newborn "creature" in me, which is what St. Paul called our spiritual self that I had miraculously given birth to that day in my mother's kitchen.

I just couldn't get enough "virtue" (which is what I called the life force) to nourish my growing spiritual hunger by "working on myself" anymore; that's why I bought into the solar cult teaching that promised the energy of the Logos "imbued" with the rays of the sun. But like everything that I have done in my life, I jumped in first and paid the price later.

So it's not easy blazing one's own trail in life when one is called to one's destiny; but I can't thank Gurdjieff enough for blazing his own trail with his Fourth Way teaching, because it brought me to the "strait gate" and introduced me to the "narrow way," and for that I will forever be grateful—because, as Jesus said, few there be that find it. I found the secret way of life, and this is what makes my story so strange…

24. Cheating the Devil

In *Secret Talks with Mr. G*, a very revealing series of esoteric talks to a specially formed group of students unknown to all of Gurdjieff's other groups, and which were recollected in private and put together to the best of their ability by these students because Gurdjieff did not allow note-taking during his talks, Gurdjieff said:

"Ordinary man has no soul. Only in the course of life is it possible for him to acquire a soul. A soul is a great luxury beyond what is provided by nature and is possible only for a few. For all ordinary manifestations a soul is not necessary.

"A soul cannot be born from nothing. It is material as is everything existing, although it is formed of a very fine matter. In order to acquire a soul it is first necessary to accumulate the required substance..." (*Secret Talks with Mr. G,* p. 124).

This is the central idea of Gurdjieff's teaching, and although in his later life he does not focus so much on this central idea but rather on waking man up from the "hypnotic sleep of life" because the naked idea of not having an immortal soul scared the bejesus out of most people, it is this idea that is pivotal to understanding Gurdjieff's teaching, an idea that I took to heart despite the fact that I could not fully embrace it.

I had been "pre-conditioned" to not fully embrace Gurdjieff's idea, because I had at least four past-life recollection dreams in my teens before I came upon Ouspensky's book *In Search of the Miraculous* in my second year at university that introduced me to Gurdjieff's teaching, and I had a pre-conscious awareness of my pre-existing self; but something about "creating" one's own soul fascinated me. It was as though I sensed in Gurdjieff's teaching a means by which I could realize my true self, and it didn't really matter to me if the premise of his teaching was true or false; all that mattered was that in his teaching of "work on oneself" I had found a path to my true self, and that's all I ever wanted from the day I made myself a promise to find my true self or die trying.

After years of reading all the literature I could get my hands on that I felt relevant to my quest, I explored the Edgar Cayce literature more deeply; and in *Intimates Through Time, Edgar Cayce's Mysteries of Reincarnation* by Jess Stearn, Edgar Cayce, the "sleeping prophet" said to be America's greatest psychic, was asked the following question: "Does every human being have a soul?"

And Cayce "replied with a simplicity that advanced a provocative concept of not only humanity's relation with God, but of God himself: 'Every human being has a soul, that which makes it akin to the Creator, that which is given an individual that he may become a companion to the Creator. As we see in the forces all about us, nature herself desires companionship. So does God, who created it all. He gives us the opportunity to be his companion, by giving us a soul, which we may make a companion to him. *But we have to do the making*'" (*Intimates Through Time*, Jess Stearn, italics mine, p.55).

"*But we have to do the making.*" This is why the merciful law of divine synchronicity brought Gurdjieff into my life; because with Gurdjieff's teaching I could "make" myself; or, as Gurdjieff expressed it within the paradigm of his own teaching, I could "create" my own soul and become a "companion to the Creator."

Edgar Cayce tapped into the Universal Mind when he went into a trance, and what the Universal Mind revealed about man's soul being a "companion to the Creator" I had proven for myself with my seven past-life regressions, which revealed to me that we all come from God as un-self-realized souls that are given the opportunity to evolve through life to acquire our own individual identity—a new "I" of God; and through the merciful twin laws of karma and reincarnation we grow in our own identity until nature has evolved us enough to take evolution into our own hands and we become conscious of our own immortal nature, as I did that miraculous day in my mother's kitchen. But what made my spiritual rebirth possible was Gurdjieff's teaching; and this brings me to what Gurdjieff called "the way of the sly man."

"The way of the sly man" is a very secret part of Gurdjieff's teaching, which to my knowledge no other student of Gurdjieff's teaching has ever given proper definition; and the reason for this, I honestly believe, is because none of Gurdjieff's students ever grasped the essential principle of "the way of the sly man"—at least not in any of the books that I have read on Gurdjieff and his teaching, and I have a whole library on Gurdjieff.

Not one student has ever explained what "the way of the sly man" is, but Gurdjieff gave us a clue in *Secret Talks with Mr. G* when he tells us that a soul needs energy to grow; but that's all it is—a clue; and although I slowly became aware of "the way of the sly man" as I "worked" on myself with *conscious effort* and *intentional suffering* (living my *Royal Dictum*, practicing Gurdjieff's techniques of *self-remembering* and *non-identifying*, as well as Christ's transformative sayings), I never really awakened to the mysterious exchange of psychic energies between people until I had my past life regression to my first primordial human lifetime when I gave birth to my reflective self, and I cannot explain "the way of the sly man" until I explain what I experienced in that lifetime—and I call it my first human life simply because I gave birth to a new "I" of God in that lifetime which is what separates man from the lower species—i.e., our reflective self-consciousness.

In my novel *Cathedral of My Past Lives* I call myself "Grunt" in my first primordial human life, because I grunted all the time to keep my small clan of ten or twelve members obedient and subservient to me, eating first and having sex whenever the urge possessed me; and if they did not heed my power grunts, I beat them savagely.

This is how I appropriated their will-to-be and grew in the consciousness of my constellating reflective self; and after carefully studying the transcript of my regression to my first primordial human lifetime, I realized that the will-to-be is the constellated life force that we take in with life experience. Being the alpha male of my clan, I had power over everyone; and as they forfeited their will-to-be to me I grew faster in my own will-to-be, until I constellated enough will-to-be to give birth to my own reflective self-consciousness. And then I realized that life experience collects the life force, which is the consciousness of life, and that the consciousness of life is the un-self-realized "I" of God; and then the puzzle became clear to me—*the reflective self is the individuated consciousness of God!*

In a word, our reflective self-consciousness is the individuated *I Am* consciousness of God that all of nature strives to give birth to, which I experienced in my first primordial human lifetime with the birth of a new "I" of God; and from lifetime to lifetime, I grew in my reflective self-consciousness through the natural individuation process of karma and reincarnation until nature could do no more for me—which speaks to the ancient alchemist's saying, "Man must complete what nature cannot finish." That's why I found Gurdjieff.

Gurdjieff maintained that nature can only evolve us so far and no further, and to complete what nature cannot finish he said that we have to take evolution into our own hands, which we could do with his teaching of "work on oneself." In effect, Gurdjieff believed that nature only gave us the potential for an immortal soul; but to realize our own immortal soul we have to "work" on ourselves with *conscious effort* and *intentional suffering* until we acquire enough life force (the *I Am* consciousness of God) to realize our immortal self, but we could speed up the process if we learned the secret "way of the sly man."

In his talks to his pupils, which Ouspensky recorded in his book *In Search of the Miraculous*, Gurdjieff said: "The fourth way is sometimes called *the way of the sly man.* The 'sly man' knows some secret which the fakir, the monk, and the yogi do not know. How the 'sly man' learned this secret—it is not known. Perhaps he found it in some old books, perhaps he inherited it, perhaps he bought it, perhaps he stole it from someone. It makes no difference. The 'sly man' knows the secret, and with its help outstrips the fakir, the monk, and the yogi" (*In Search of the Miraculous*, P. D. Ouspensky, p. 50).

I found out what this secret was, but I did not find out from any person, as such; nor did I find out from any book, as such; nor did I steal it from anyone, as such. I came upon the secret by "working on myself" in my daily interactions with life, because the more I tried to transform myself with *conscious effort* and *intentional suffering* the more I became aware of the shadow self of man, or what Gurdjieff called one's "false personality."

Remember, I had heard a voice in my mind asking me why I lied, and I became acutely conscious of my own falseness which activated Gurdjieff's technique of *self-remembering* that made me very conscious of everything that I thought, said, and did; so I was determined to make conscious efforts in my daily life to be as honest and fair and truthful as I could be, and this made me more and more conscious of the false personality in others. And the more conscious I became of my own falseness and the falseness of others, the more I began to notice the psychic play of energies between people; and by psychic energy, I mean that precious life force that we need to grow in our own identity.

It was this play of psychic energies between people that alerted me to "the way of the sly man." I had to master the art of spiritual survival in my daily affairs with life; because the more I lost my precious life force to another, the less life force I had to grow in my own self-identity—which I desperately needed to *become* my true self. And even though I became a master of the secret way of the "sly" man, which simply meant that I learned how to not forfeit my precious life force to other people, it wasn't until I studied Jung's psychology of the personality and shadow self that I put it all together.

The shadow is the unconscious side of our ego personality, and it is the self of our *non-being*, the self of our unresolved ego personality which makes it non-real and false. But as I've already explained, although our unconscious shadow is non-real, it is the self of our *non-being* and very real in itself; and because it is real in itself, it also needs energy to grow in its own identity. And this is where life gets very tricky, because the shadow will steal another person's life force with guile, deception, and even intimidation—like the husband who threatens his wife to do what he says, or else.

And not only does the shadow steal the life force from other people with guile, deception, and intimidation; it steals it from its own ego personality as well. This is why Jesus admonished us to do our good in silence and not vaunt it publically, because as we boast about the good we have done (goodness is the "virtue" of life, the precious life force that has been realized either through excellence or giving of oneself unselfishly), we forfeit it to our shadow self that needs it for its own survival. But the more honest, fair, and truthful that I tried to be, the less power my shadow had over me—and the shadow self of life as well.

Jung called the unconscious shadow self of life the Archetypal Shadow, which is the collective shadow self of every person in the world—alive and dead; which makes the Archetypal Shadow the False One, or what Christianity calls the Devil. And if the Archetypal Shadow is the Devil, then our personal shadow is our own private devil that we have created out of the unresolved energy of our ego personality. This is what Robert Louis Stevenson captured with his novel *The Strange Case of Dr. Jekyll and Mr. Hyde.*

In effect, we all have a little Mr. Hyde in us; and we nourish and sustain our private devil by being false and dishonest with ourselves and other people. And learning how to cheat the Devil of the precious life force that I needed to grow in my own immortal nature (as Gurdjieff put it, I was "creating" my own soul), I had to learn the art of spiritual survival—which meant being as wise as a serpent and innocent as a dove.

That's how I became a "sly" man.

25. Awakened Conscience

I wish I had the courage to write about my sexual experience that catapulted me into my spiritual quest, but I don't; and if ever I do summon the courage, you can rest assured that I would couch it in fiction, because that's the only way I could ever do it justice. But even fiction would be worrisome, because the author would still be stigmatized; like the American writer Philip Roth was stigmatized by the masturbatory fantasies in his novel *Portnoy's Complaint* that launched his literary career. I dread to think of what it cost him personally.

But it wasn't my sexual experience in itself that was so heinous (if that's the right word, which I don't think it is; perhaps morally disconcerting would be more fitting), but the humiliating context of my experience which I had to live with. That's why I fled to France, to get away from everyone and everything that reminded me of what I had done.

My sexual experience traumatized me. It shocked my conscience awake and brutalized me emotionally, mentally, and spiritually. *How could I possible do that?* And it gave me little comfort to know that the person who did what he did that night was not me, but another me that I did not even know existed; that's why I had to go on my quest for my true self—just as my high school poem *Noman* had foretold six years earlier.

In my poem, God summoned Noman (which was me) for a reckoning, and I was found wanting; and God condemned me to the "fourth corner of the abyss" to find my lost soul. I had no idea what my poem meant, and it took me many years to figure out what my unconscious was telling me; but when I shocked my conscience awake with my sexual experience that night after closing my pool hall for the day, I found myself in the Court of God just as I was standing in the Court of God when God found Noman wanting; and I condemned myself to the task of finding my true self or die trying. That's why I divested myself of my business interests and fled to France to begin my quest for my lost soul.

Gurdjieff Was Wrong But His Teaching Works

Upon reflection all these many years later, having successful completed my quest for my lost soul, I know now that no soul is ever lost as such; it's just mired so deep in the consciousness of one's *non-being* that one's perspective is completely distorted, and one cannot see the wood for the trees—like Macbeth in Shakespeare's play. If I may, let me quote Macbeth's famous soliloquy that inspired my first literary effort in Annecy, France:

To-morrow, and to-morrow, and to-morrow,
Creeps in this petty pace from day to day,
To the last syllable of recorded time;
And all our yesterdays have lighted fools
The way to dusty death. Out, out, brief candle!
Life's but a walking shadow, a poor player,
That struts and frets his hour upon the stage,
And then is heard no more. It is a tale
Told by an idiot, full of sound and fury,
Signifying nothing.

I called my first literary effort *This Petty Pace*, because I was so deeply mired in the consciousness of my own nothingness—which is a philosophical way of saying that my "I", or ego self, was centered in the *non-being* aspect of my *being*, or false self; but because of my sexual experience that shocked my conscience awake, I could not suffer myself and had to find a way to redeem myself from my own nothingness.

That was my quest, which I could never have fulfilled without Gurdjieff's teaching of "work on oneself" that taught me how to transform the consciousness of my false self; but not without the help of my *Royal Dictum*, and the sayings of Jesus.

I was a brutally traumatized young man when I went to France, and very confused when I got there, and especially after my meditation experience that accidentally awakened the "serpent fire" that set my mind ablaze with wild, undisciplined sexual energy; but I know now that my life was being guided by an agency that I have to call divine.

Whether it was my Higher Self, Divine Spirit, or simply God, I don't know; but I was given an insight into the life I had destined myself to live by a piece of prophetically inspired writing that came out of me one melancholy afternoon when I came in from a long walk in the snow. I was so tired, so confused, so scared, and so lonely that I didn't know what to do; and I picked up my pen and wrote the following words that burned themselves into my memory because they came from the deepest depths of my tortured soul; and although I have already quoted these words in Chapter 4, I have to repeat them to emphasize that without an awakened conscience we can never realize our destiny to our true self:

Steadfast and courageous is he, who having overcome woe and grief remains alone and undaunted; alone I say, for to be otherwise would hardly seem possible, for one must bear one's conscience alone. He must fight the battle and win the battle, odds or no odds. He must win to establish the equilibrial tranquility of body and soul, and sooner or later he will erupt as a volcano of unlimited confidence which will purpose his life thereafter. And having given birth to such magnificence, he will no longer be alone alone, but alone in society; and he will see the mirror of his puerile grief in the eyes of his fellow man.

I learned later that there is no such word as "equilibrial", but that's the word that my creative unconscious took poetic license to create, and I'm not going to change it because it describes the harmonizing tranquility that I had to establish between my body and soul, which spoke to the relentless efforts that I would have to make to tame the "serpent fire" and resolve the conflict in my soul between my shadow and ego personality. Is it any wonder that Gurdjieff was drawn into my life with his teaching of self-transformation? I was called to his teaching by an inner imperative, and I was *compelled* to live by it to find my true self.

But I would never have been called to transform my false self had I not had that sexual experience that brutally shocked my conscience awake, because as long as I stayed asleep to my shadow self I would have continued living my life under what Gurdjieff called the "hypnotic spell of life" and remained oblivious to my unconscious shadow. And this was Gurdjieff's gift to me—waking me up to what he called my "false personality."

Gurdjieff Was Wrong But His Teaching Works

We all have a false self, which is the self of our *non-being*; and whether we like it or not, we're all affected by our unconscious falseness. But as I took Gurdjieff's teaching out into the marketplace with my house-painting business, I began to see just how much power my false self had over me; and I had to muster all the moral courage that I could just to be honest with my customers and everyone else—and most especially, with myself.

That's how I "worked" on myself with Gurdjieff's teaching of *conscious effort* and *intentional suffering*, because it cost me every time my false self wanted to cut corners in my work or cheat my customers by lying and overcharging them. It was hard to be honest in my painting business because it was so easy to lie and cheat my customers, and although I'm not proud to say that I was less than honest every now and then when I couldn't help myself, I finally managed to get my moral bearings and made integrity my personal ethic.

But had I not shocked my conscience awake with my traumatizing sexual experience that godforsaken night, I would not have had a moral compass to guide me in my quest for my true self; because whenever my false self wanted to possess me, my conscience came to my defense and I fought with myself until I won. That's how I wrestled my own little devil to the ground and shifted my center of gravity from my false to my true self.

26. To Be, or Not to Be?

Although I had a pre-conscious awareness of my false self because of all the literature that I had read (aside from catching myself in my own falseness, that is; which I usually repressed to my unconscious because I did not want to deal with my falseness consciously until I discovered Gurdjieff's teaching of "work on oneself"), Shakespeare's *Hamlet* and stories like *The Picture of Dorian Gray* by Oscar Wilde, and especially *The Strange Case of Dr. Jekyll and Mr. Hyde* by Robert Louis Stevenson, I was delightfully surprised to see that Gurdjieff had made the dual consciousness of man central to his teaching in what he called man's *essence* and *personality*—the two aspects of our *being* and *non-being*.

Gurdjieff tells us in Ouspensky's book *In Search of the Miraculous*: *"Essence is the truth in man; personality is the false."* In effect, *essence* is what we are born with; and *personality* is what we create because of social conditioning—which I accept without reservation; but I have expanded upon this perspective because of my belief in karma and reincarnation. This esoteric spiritual perspective gives me the larger picture of the dual consciousness of man, and it's from this larger perspective that I can tell my story.

But it was Gurdjieff's teaching of *essence* and *personality* that got me started, because without his penetrating insight into the dual consciousness of man I would never have seen the distinction between my *being* and *non-being*. Actually I had already sensed this distinction, only too acutely because of my sexual experience that brutally shocked my conscience awake; but, as life goes, it's all about timing. Which simply meant that I was ready to take evolution into my own hands and complete what nature could not finish. That's why the merciful law of divine synchronicity brought Gurdjieff's teaching into my life.

"A very important moment in the work on oneself is when a man begins to distinguish between his personality and his essence," said Gurdjieff. "A man's real I, his individuality, can grow only from his essence. It can be said that a man's individuality is his essence grown up, mature. But in order to enable essence to grow up, it is first of all necessary to weaken the constant pressure of personality upon it, because the obstacles to the growth of essence are contained in personality" (*In Search of the Miraculous*, P. D. Ouspensky, p. 163).

This was my entry point into Gurdjieff's teaching of self-transformation, because now I had a conceptual framework to give my life the direction it needed to find my true self, because according to Gurdjieff I could only grow in my real "I" by growing in my *essence*, which would be at the expense of my *personality*—hence my instinctive attraction to Gurdjieff's dynamic principle of "work on oneself." And from day to day I practiced the techniques of *self-remembering* and *non-identifying* to transform the consciousness of my personality and grow in my real "I", which was how I "created" my own soul.

As effective as Gurdjieff's teaching was however, I could not have "created" my own soul without the help of my *Royal Dictum* and the sayings of Jesus which intensified the natural process of my individuation; but this is how life works in any event.

All Gurdjieff did with his teaching was speed up the natural individuation process of our *essence*, or real "I", and I know this with gnostic certainty because I worked it out many years after I gave birth to my spiritual self in my mother's kitchen and Penny and I moved to Georgian Bay where I had seven past-life regressions that opened up a window onto the Divine Plan of God that let me see soul's evolution through life.

As I've already written, soul comes into the world as an un-self-realized atom of God that evolves through the multifarious stages of life until it has evolved enough in a higher species to give birth to a new "I" of God, which I experienced in my regression to the Body of God where we all come from and my first primordial human lifetime as a higher primate when I experienced the dawning of my reflective self; and from lifetime to lifetime, the newborn "I" of God evolves until the natural process of karma and reincarnation can evolve soul no further, and then one has to take evolution into their own hands to complete what nature cannot finish—which I can confirm with my own experience with Gurdjieff's teaching and the birth of my spiritual self in my mother's kitchen. That's how I know that Gurdjieff's teaching works, despite his premise that man is not born with an immortal soul.

But the irony of Gurdjieff's remarkable teaching, which he spent twenty years and more to find and put together out of all the hidden mystery teachings that he had scoured Central Asia and the Far East to find, is that there is nothing really secret about it; or, rather, the same teaching of spiritual rebirth can be found in Christ's teaching, Sufism, and Taoism to name the most obvious—and in the very process of life itself, actually!

This is the deep mystery of life, which in itself is the way to our true self; meaning, the very experience of living life is how we grow in the individuating consciousness of our *essence*. But, sadly, nature can only individuate our *essence* so much, and no more; which is why when one feels that life can no longer satisfy the longing in their soul they suffer the despair that Shakespeare so eloquently described in Hamlet's epic soliloquy—

To be, or not to be: that is the question;
Whether 'tis nobler in the mind to suffer
The slings and arrows of outrageous fortune,
Or to take arms against a sea of troubles,
And by opposing end them? To die: to sleep;
No more; and by a sleep to say we end
The heart-ache and the thousand natural shocks
That flesh is heir to, 'tis a consummation
Devoutly to be wish'd. To die, to sleep'
To sleep: perchance to dream: ay, there's the rub;
For in that sleep of death what dreams may come
When we have shuffled off this mortal coil,
Must give us pause: there's the respect
That makes calamity of so long life;
For who would bear the whips and scorns of time,
The oppressor's wrong, the proud man's contumely,
The pangs of despised love, the law's delay,
The insolence of office and the spurns
That patient merit of the unworthy takes,
When he himself might his quietus make
With a bare bodkin? who would fardels bear,

Gurdjieff Was Wrong But His Teaching Works

To grunt and sweat under a weary life,
But that the dread of something after death,
The undiscovered country from whose bourn
No traveller returns, puzzles the will
And makes us rather bear those ills we have
Than fly to others that we know not of?
Thus conscience doth make cowards of us all;
And thus the native hue of resolution
Is sicklied o'er with the pale castoff thought,
And enterprises of great pitch and moment
With this regard their currents turn awry,
And lose the name of action.

Hamlet has come as far as nature can take him through the natural process of individuation, and he's stuck in the no-man's land of his tortured soul; and he despairs. Does he end it all by taking his own life, avenge his father's murder, or does he continue to suffer the indignities of "Old Whore Life"? What's the point of it all, anyway? Is life a tale told by an idiot full of sound and fury signifying nothing? If so, why go on? That's Hamlet's dilemma.

And that's the kind of existential angst that I suffered when I wrote my first novel in Annecy, France which I called *This Petty Pace;* I was trapped in the consciousness of my own *non-being*, and I despaired like the tragic Prince of Denmark.

But I had vowed to find my true self or die trying, and I returned to Canada and enrolled at Lakehead University to study philosophy, and by the second year I had grown enough in my *essence* to attract Gurdjieff into my life; and in the second semester of my third year I dropped out of university to forge my own path in life with Gurdjieff's teaching to guide me. And then I "discovered" Carl Gustav Jung, who gave me the psychological clarity that I needed to make sense of my life; but I wrote a novel that upset my hometown, and Penny and I had to relocate to Georgian Bay, and the rest, as they say, is history.

27. Gurdjieff, Jung, and Me

In Chapter 9, "The Law of Reciprocal Maintenance" in *Gurdjieff: Making a New World*, by J. G. Bennett, one of Gurdjieff's most advanced pupils, Bennett reflected the essence of Gurdjieff's remarkable teaching in the following words: "Man's nature is dynamic: in order to be, he must become. In order to become, he must pay the price of his existence. When he has done so, unlimited vistas of cosmic realization open up to him." The quest for my true self attests to this realization, beginning with my *Royal Dictum* which was the price that I chose to pay for the truth that I sought from God.

I can still remember that lonely day standing on the breakwater that separated the Nipigon River from the Nipigon Bay and marina, looking upward into the heavens and asking God "what price truth?" I knew that nothing came free in this world, and I asked God what price I had to pay to find my true self, and God replied by granting me the insights that gave birth to my edict of self-denial, which I called my *Royal Dictum*; and as I denied myself the pleasures of my life, I paid life back the price of my own existence, and "unlimited vistas of cosmic realization" opened up to me; and for that, I have Gurdjieff to thank.

If I could reduce the influence that Gurdjieff's teaching had upon me into one simple insight (not to mention the influence of Gurdjieff's image, which made such a powerful impression upon me that I feel I knew him personally; which, perhaps I did, given that I met him in my dreams several times that I remember), I would have to say that his teaching proved incontrovertibly that **TO BE, WE HAVE TO BECOME**.

Gurdjieff consciously understood the *enantiodromiac* dynamics of our *becoming*, the *being* and *non-being* aspects of our nature which he garnered from esoteric mystery schools that he found in his quest for an answer to the haunting question of his life—*"What is the sense and significance in general of life on earth, and in particular of human life?"*—and he put it all together into a teaching of self-transformation, which he called The Fourth Way; and I would agree with what A. R. Orage, another one of Gurdjieff's most advanced pupils, said about Gurdjieff's teaching, that it was "sublime common sense," except, of course, for his premise that man is not born with an immortal soul upon which his whole teaching rests.

That's the irony of Gurdjieff's teaching, because it doesn't really matter if we have an immortal soul or not, one still has to BECOME in order to BE. Which, strangely enough, is exactly what Jesus taught with his teaching: ***"He that loveth his life shall lose it; and he that hateth his life in this world shall keep it unto life eternal"*** (John, 12: 25). Given this, it's easy to believe why Gurdjieff would call his teaching "esoteric Christianity."

To grow in our essential self, which is the source of our own individuality, the "I" of who we are, we have to transform the consciousness of our personality, which is the "I" of who we are not—our false self; and in this transformation we *become* our true self. This is the gist of Gurdjieff's teaching; everything else is information, and however fascinating it may be (and it is), it bears little relevance to our *becoming*. That's why I could never get pulled into Gurdjieff's *All and Everything* that purports to adjust our perspective on human nature and wake us up from the "hypnotic sleep of life"—if one but have the time, patience, and determination to read it three times as Gurdjieff suggested.

But life will do that to us, anyway; because this is the natural way of the *enantiodromiac* process of our *becoming*. Even vernacular expressions speak to this process; like, "Wake up and smell the coffee." Or simple expostulations, like "Wake up, for Christ's sake!" And didn't Jesus admonish his disciples to "wake up"? But wake up from what?

From our own false consciousness, that's what; from our own *non-being*, which casts a shadow upon our life that distorts our perspective on realty—or the way things really are; like the husband who is blind to his wife's affair with his best friend. All of their friends can see it, but not him; he's blind to the reality of his marital situation, and not until he catches his wife in bed with his best friend will he wake up to the reality.

"There are none so blind as those who refuse to see," says the old adage; which speaks to the hold that our unconscious can have upon us, and waking up to life is really waking up from the hold that our own unconscious has upon us. That's what living Gurdjieff's teaching did for me; it woke me up to my unconscious self as I "worked" on myself, because "working" on myself transformed the consciousness of my false self, and I *became* more real—so real, in fact, that my very presence began to chafe people.

The more real one becomes (which simply means that one grounds himself more in his essential nature than his ego personality), the more grounded he is in reality, or the essential truth of life; and, as Carl Jung realized, he can become a force of nature, as he tells us in his own words in *Wounded Healer of the Soul*: "It is the truth, a force of nature that expresses itself through me—I am only a channel—I can imagine in many instances where I would become sinister to you. For instance, if life has led you to take up an artificial attitude, than you wouldn't be able to stand me, because I am a natural being. By my very presence I crystallize; I am a ferment. The unconscious of people who live in an artificial manner senses me as a danger. Everything about me irritates them, my way of speaking, my way of laughing. They sense nature" (*Wounded Healer of the Soul*, Claire Dunne, p. 22).

I can vouchsafe this, because I can also irritate people just with my presence alone (and some of my spiritual musings given some comments that I have received); but there's an obverse side to this phenomenon, which Jung must have known but never expressed as clearly as the chafing effect he had upon certain people; at least, not that I am aware of in all the books that I have read by him and about him, and that has to do with the attracting factor of one's nature (one's personal energy) that pulls people, especially children who are still grounded in their essential nature, into their field of energy like bees to honey—especially Gurdjieff, who had so much gravitas that he was like a dynamo of animal magnetism.

In a word, the more real one is the more he will either attract or repel you, depending upon your own nature. That is, the more one is grounded in their *non-being*, or false nature, the more they will be repelled by one whose is centered in his *being*, or essential nature; and the more one is grounded in their *being*, or essential nature, the more they will be attracted to one who has more gravitas, someone like Jung or Gurdjieff who were magnificent specimens of paradoxically balanced, self-fulfilled individuals, which is why I loved them both.

Gurdjieff Was Wrong But His Teaching Works

Gurdjieff influenced me much more than Jung, but Jung would have meant nothing to me had I not lived Gurdjieff's teaching; and what Jung did for me was put my life into proper perspective. Jung was a spiritual person who lived the secret way, but he couched what he learned about human nature in the language of psychology because he did not want to risk the scientific credibility of his budding new discipline of Analytical Psychology; and as far as I can tell, Carl Gustav Jung learned so much about the individuation process of man's *becoming* that it will take society at least another twenty-five to fifty years to catch up to him, and he may come unto his own by the year 2050. It's for this reason that I believe he will be remembered and studied long after Gurdjieff is gathering dust on the shelves of esoteric literature—and all because Gurdjieff founded his teaching upon a premise that is inconsistent with the reality of man's spiritual nature, which Jung embraced implicitly.

As Jesus said in Glenda Green's book *The Keys of Jeshua,* **"there is nothing but the self and God,"** which as far as I can tell is the fundamental premise of Jung's psychology of individuation; and as I bring my strange story to closure, I have to thank George Ivanovich Gurdjieff for initiating me into this glorious mystery, because without his teaching of "work on oneself" I would never have found my true self, and looked into the Face of God.

Thank you, my one and only true teacher.

About the Author

Orest Stocco was born in Calabria, Italy. He emmigrated to Canada and studied philosophy at university. A student of Gurdjieff's teaching for many years, his passion for writing inspired such works as *The Summoning of Noman* and *The Pearl of Great Price.* He lives in Georgian Bay, Ontario with his life mate Penny Lynn Cates. His personal dictum is: Life is an individual journey.
Visit him at: http://ostocco.wix.com/ostocco
Spiritual Musings Blog:
http://www.spiritualmusingsbyoreststocco.blogspot.com

ME AND MY SISPYHEAN ROCK

www.ingramcontent.com/pod-product-compliance
Lightning Source LLC
LaVergne TN
LVHW011417080426
835512LV00005B/120